Biblical Le

MW01272934

Biblical Leadership:
The Fifth Frame

A Model of Leadership for Every Christian

Tony Metze

ISBN : 1-4196-4655-9

To order additional copies, please contact us.
BookSurge, LLC
www.booksurge.com
1-866-308-6235
orders@booksurge.com

Biblical Leadership: The Fifth Frame

Table of Contents

Foreword

Thirteen years ago, I started attending a monthly magic meeting with Tony Metze. Throughout these years we would ride together to the meetings and have several hours to discuss various subjects. Many times the conversation would be about leadership. Personal, familial, and business leadership would be discussed. Church work is important to both of us. Many times we compared our churches to being a family and a business in itself. Leading a family or a business can be very similar.

In "the Fifth Frame" Tony shows how Christian Leadership can be modified to lead families and churches. Tony deals effectively with both the complexities and ambiguities that pop up when ever we become involved with leadership in the church.

Tony uses both modern and biblical leaders as examples; from Moses & Jesus to Sam Walton & Jack Welch to show various leadership styles. He brings out his experiences as a father, husband and pastor to show a clear path of leadership when dealing with life's problems.

Personally, I describe Tony as a goal driven visionary. Whether he is balancing a difficult situation in the church or showing a child a magic trick; Tony teaches and counsels with kindness and compassion. Tony leads by example and has the patience to follow through with the necessary details to make things happen. He is not afraid to allow people to find their own way. Tony is both generous with praise and teaching. He creates leadership abilities in others.

I am proud to call Tony my friend. Read and enjoy "the Fifth Frame". Learn from a disciplined visionary who shows compassion for people and yet instructs and teaches.

Bobby Jonte

Preface

I love the church and the Lord of the Church—Jesus Christ. My entire life is marked by involvement in the work of God's holy church. Little did I know that my years in high school and college working with youth, serving on council, and making stewardship visits was God's preparation for me as a parish pastor. I am a blessed man and am thankful to serve the church. What I have learned in twenty one years of ordained ministry is very simple. To be a parish pastor, one must lead. As my military parishioners say, "Lead, follow, or get out of the way."

Clergy and laity must lead all the time. There is no time for a break. As Kenneth Haugk proposes in his book, *Antagonist in the Church*, "Weakness invites and strength repels." A weak leader invites trouble, while a strong leader will repel it. How can pastors and parishioners be strong leaders? That is the ultimate question addressed in this book. One day in the midst of research for my doctoral dissertation, I had the insight that church leaders do not need another text on leadership, but a model of *Christian* leadership. While secular leadership books and studies are an immense help, they are insufficient without more.

Christian leaders need a model designed specifically for them that incorporates the best of secular ideas, but encases it in a biblical frame. This, "The Fifth Frame" is that model. It is so named because it builds on the four frames explained in *Reframing Organizations* by Lee Bolman and Terrence Deal.

No one writes a book alone. While it is true that I hammered the keyboard for countless hours crafting this book, my experiences and ideas is the result of interactions with numerous people. First, I am extremely grateful to Dr. Lee Bolman who not only responded to my initial email to him, but also provided a leadership inventory for my doctoral research. Secondly, I must thank Dr. Steve Klipowiz, my dissertation advisor, who encouraged me when hope was withering. I also owe a debt of gratitude to three South Carolina Lutheran congregations (Good Shepherd, Faith, and St. James) who taught me how to be a pastor.

I owe a special thank you to the eight pastors of my test group who took the leadership inventory, enlisted lay persons to do the same, answered in-depth interview questions, and provided theological reflections that helped me formulate my thoughts. Pastors Richard Campbell, Julian Gordy, Richard Goeres, Christopher Fischer, Roger Lindler, Patrick Riddle, Howard Sale, and Ralph Stillwell showed deep love for Christ and the church in helping with this project. Also, a huge thank you is extended to the one hundred and twenty five pastors and fifty seven lay persons that participated in the leadership project.

Unsung heroes include my editors, Mr. Paul Culotta and Rev. Elizabeth Platts, who provided me insight and editing help throughout. Where there is error, count that to me; where there is clarity, credit my editing team.

Most importantly, I thank my family for their support and encouragement. My mother, wife, daughter, and twin sons are God's treasures to me. Feedback from my daughter's Religion colloquium at Newberry College helped me refine a few points, but the biggest gift from all my family has been the sharing of life's daily joys and the solving of life's daily conundrums.

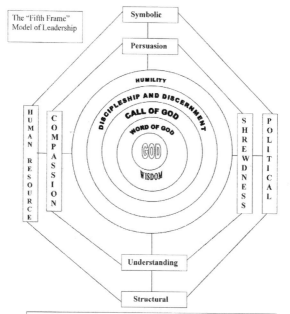

The "Fifth Frame" Model of Leadership

Symbolic

Persuasion

HUMILITY

DISCIPLESHIP AND DISCERNMENT

CALL OF GOD

WORD OF GOD

GOD

WISDOM

HUMAN RESOURCE

COMPASSION

SHREWDNESS

POLITICAL

Understanding

Structural

"BEING"
God, Word of God, Wisdom, Call of God, Discipleship and Discernment, Humility
"BECOMING"
Persuasion, Shrewdness, Understanding, Compassion
"DOING"
Symbolic, Political, Structural, Human Resource

Introduction

Why Christian Leadership?

This afternoon you received a phone call from the church office. The pastor wants you to lead the evangelism team. A host of excuses race through your mind, deepening your resolve to say "No." Aside from your fear of doing the job well, you are uncertain of how to integrate what you know about leadership with the leadership dynamics of the congregation. Is there really a difference? Are your perceptions, knowledge, and styles of leadership applicable to the church? What does it mean to lead a Christian evangelism team?

Defining Christian leadership is a question that has plagued me since the day I graduated from seminary. Just what does it mean to be a Christian leader? My journey began in high school. The place was Spartanburg High School study hall. Rick and I were discussing our future, what would we do? Where would we go to college? In a rare moment of self-disclosure, I shared my interest in church work and the possibility of being a pastor. The thought of ministry was a faint and distant idea, but it still lingered in my mind.

Nine years later I listened with an overwhelming sense of awe as the congregation at Wiles auditorium, Newberry College, broke into thunderous applause. Six hundred plus representatives of the South Carolina Synod of the Lutheran Church in America were gathered for the annual convention. Scripture was read, vows were taken, and hands were placed upon our heads. Three other men and I were ordained as pastors of Christ's Church.

Two months later I arrived at Good Shepherd Lutheran Church in Swansea, South Carolina. The town population was 681. Although the town and church were small, the leadership challenge was great. How would I preach every Sunday, make the necessary visits, and most importantly, how would I lead these people? Seminary had taught me much about teaching the scripture, leading worship, and counseling, but I felt ill prepared to lead.

The first challenge came quite unexpectedly. Jane Ann, our organist, noticed that First Baptist Church of Batesburg, South Carolina had a pipe organ for sale. Although she was young, only 16 at the time, and there was no demonstrated need for a new instrument, she had a grand vision for the music of the church. Excitedly, she and I drove to Batesburg to see the instrument. We talked with the Baptist pastor who said the asking price was only one thousand dollars but there was a huge extra cost to move it. I could not wait to ask our church council for permission to buy this beautiful 1933 Moeller pipe organ. Naturally, the council was skeptical, but the members also raised very practical concerns. For instance, where would we put it? I had a clear vision, but had not bothered to realize that the worship space of a church built in 1912 had no place for a pipe organ of this magnitude. After deliberation, the council met and decided not to take the organ unless it was given to us. I was saddened but understood their concerns.

The next morning the pastor at First Baptist of Batesburg called. The next few words from him were nothing short of divine intervention. Unaware of our meeting or our decision he said, "We met last night and decided to give the organ to your congregation."

He asked us to take up a love offering for their ministry and to move the instrument. I made numerous phone calls to council members and they all agreed to move the organ. A number of men of the congregation gathered one Saturday morning with tools, trucks, and camera. The camera proved to be a most helpful idea. Pictures were made of the entire organ and the wiring. Wilson, a member with a large empty barn, agreed to store the organ until the congregation could make a final decision about how to install the organ. Once it was moved there were more pitfalls along the way. We had to build a balcony just to house the instrument, but there was no money to do it.

One year later a congregational meeting was held to figure out what to do with the organ we had moved and stored for the past year in Wilson's garage. The mood was cautious and I could see this dream going up in smoke. What would a Christian leader do? As Lila, the church council president, opened the discussion and noted that we had no money to build a balcony – one by one individual's stood up pledging money to build the balcony. Jerry, an adult whom I had baptized, started it off with $600 dollars. Before the meeting ended, Lila held nearly two thousand three hundred dollars in her hands. A miracle had occurred.

Dick, a member and construction company owner, recruited a crew and built a balcony just to house the instrument. Construction in the 1912 facility proved quite a challenge. When all was put together and the organ reassembled using the pictures we had made, the organ would not play. We were horrified. We called an organ builder from Charlotte, North Carolina. In less than two days work at a very reasonable price, he had the organ playing beautifully. A dedication was held and the organ plays to this day. It is a small church that had a big dream mingled with the mighty hand of God.

This was my first major experience in leading a congregation to do something seemingly out of their reach. What were the tasks of leadership in this experience? There were many, including, vision, persuasion, perseverance, a belief in the people of God, and also a firm belief in God's miraculous power. Many days, especially during the year the organ was in storage, I asked if my dream for a pipe organ was from God or just my wishful thinking. My prayers were ones of trust as I had come to believe that God's will would prevail.

Though I had lived through the experience and managed to exercise some form of leadership through it all, I floundered to define just what Christian leadership was. Now, after twenty years of experience as an ordained pastor in the Lutheran Church, I am convinced that a necessary component of vibrant congregations is strong Christian leadership. The need for leadership is as great today as ever. Herb Miller writes, "Leadership is not everything in growing a congregation, but it is the something without which little else happens."[1] In every present instance of church renewal and even in the historical examples of the past, strong leadership is the catalyst.

Nothing has convinced me of this more than the current malaise affecting my own denomination. There are more conflicts and special interest groups than any other previous time. While there is much success in the Lutheran Church, there is also a frustrating lack of identity. Imagine my surprise at the following words from a 1958 issue of Look magazine:

> The Lutherans exemplify the present revival of religious interest. In the ten years 1946 – 1956, they increased by 1,716,592 (in 1956 their total U.S. membership was 7,388,176).[2] This gain is comprised primarily of converts, who have found the clear-cut, uncompromising doctrines of Martin Luther, founder of the Reformation, a message suited to modern needs. The new converts have not, however, just walked in the door. They have been recruited by brisk, up to the minute methods. With imagination and fervor, the Lutherans have adapted twentieth – century techniques to Gospel preaching. This evangelistic surge is of rather recent origin. The entire denomination has come alive, as though it had suddenly decided to make good President Theodore Roosevelt's 53-year old prophesy that 'the Lutheran Church is destined to become one of the two or three greatest and most important churches in the United States.'[3]

Unfortunately, the bright prediction of President Theodore Roosevelt in 1903 never came to pass for Lutherans or other mainline churches. There are dark clouds hovering over our denominations. Why has membership declined?

Church scholars have proposed a number of theories for the decline of the mainline denominations such as the theory that mainline churches became weak as religious bodies due to their allowance for a diversity of theological viewpoints.[4] Reflecting on this thesis Benton Johnson concluded that mainline churches are unable to generate and maintain high levels of commitment.[5] In essence you get what you expect. If nothing is expected of individuals when they join a congregation, then an apathetic culture will prevail. Eventually a congregation could find itself evolving into noninvolvement.

One church newsletter conveyed this sense of noninvolvement with the story of a mythical family known as the "somebody else family." The writer commented that many members often said let "somebody else" do it. The plight of the paid clergy is that many church people believe that ministry is only done by the paid professionals. While adding staff is a sure way to assist in the growth of a congregation, adding disciples with core orthodox values of faith and high commitment is certain to grow a congregation spiritually and by God's will and grace numerically as well.

The presence of a core value of orthodoxy is important. According to the study by Johnson orthodox Christian belief was the best predictor of church participation, whereas a "pick and choose" pattern of belief elicited the most erosion of commitment.[6] What this means is churches that adhered to foundational orthodox beliefs and had high expectations of members had better overall participation from their membership.

Another theory offered by Herb Miller suggests there are four spiritual types of worshippers: thinking, action, feeling and meditative.[7] He writes, "Many people find greater benefit in a Feeling Type of spirituality during historical periods when the culture is unstable, the political order is crumbling, personal roles are poorly defined, and people feel a low sense of personal power to affect their future."[8] While mainline denominations stimulate spiritual feelings, "emotional content" as Miller refers to it, is not the center of their styles of worship. Our current world situation is a time of political, economic, and cultural unrest. According to Miller's theory this compels individuals to a "Feeling" type of spirituality. This, in turn, could hurt the more liturgical denominations.

What evidences of decline are seen in mainlines? During the height of church growth in the 1950s, not only was the evangelistic fervor stronger than ever, but mainline churches could count on denominational loyalty for retention of membership and growth. Christians who moved from one state to another almost always looked for a church of their denomination.

This no longer happens. Current generations view the church through the eyes of a consumer searching for the best brand at the best price. Foss writes, "In the Protestant explosion of the 1950s, membership implied obligation. In today's cultural context, membership has come to imply prerogatives."[9] Today people ask, "What is in it for me?" and "What do I get for my offering?" These questions override any denominational loyalty.

The consumerist attitude can affect the attitude of the clergy and their leadership as well. H. Richard Niebuhr wrote nearly fifty years ago,

> The voluntaristic system of the free churches in North America, it has been said, has tended to transform their officials into merchants who offer all sorts of wares so that as many customers as possible may be attracted to their ecclesiastical emporiums.[10]

Clergy and lay leaders are attracted to consumerist models of growth because of its prevalence in our society. Though many would argue that this is a recent development in American

Christianity, the roots of a consumerist religion began in colonial days.

Colonial American religious history was marked by a somewhat theological dominance of the Church of England. Even though there were other Christians, early settlers knew that there was little toleration for beliefs other than those of the established church. The assertiveness of Anglicans in South Carolina caused quarrels to erupt among clergy of differing denominations. Consider for example this excerpt from a letter by a Hugenot minister, John Lapierre. In this letter, Lapierre complains to the Bishop of London regarding the intolerance of South Carolina Anglicans. The letter is dated January 7, 1726. Lapierre wrote, "The Reverend Garden was my first open adversary I had in this province, upon information that I had baptised a child of one of his parishioners."[11] The Reverend Garden responded to Lapierre with very strong words. Consider the opening of his letter to Lapierre, "I have often heard of your insolent and disorderly practices in other parishes, but little suspected that I should have experienced them in my own."[12] This bitter exchange illustrates the competitiveness for members in colonial America.

The Great Awakening, a period in American religious history beginning in 1740, increased competitiveness. One major contributor was Gilbert Tennent. Tennent attacked the parish system suggesting that parishioners should not feel bound to any particular congregation simply based on geographic proximity. Rather, Tennent argued in the sermon, "The Danger of An Unconverted Ministry,"[13] that individuals should attend the congregation where they are assured that the minister is truly converted.

Consumerist religion in all its facets continues to be a threat to genuine Christian community. Robert Bacher and Kenneth Innskeep concluded their investigation into the mainline denominations with three worries regarding Christianity in the United States. Their primary concern is that it may be impossible to change consumerist religion. They contend that individuals see the church as a training center where one goes to sign up for the latest course in how to live. Sadly, most do not see the church as a community of believers who strive to do God's will.[14]

Certainly one cannot fault church members for seeking congregations to which they feel called and in which they experience a deep sense of belonging and mission. It is, however, imperative that Christian leaders be aware of market driven models of leadership. Success in organizations is often equated with numbers only and the church is no different. Is it possible that our models of leadership have come not only from the secular realm, but also are deeply rooted in early American religious history? If so, have these models hurt Christian leaders? Is it possible that our focus on leadership is on the end result and not rooted in God? Even civic leaders have become so attentive to the bottom line that they have no moral imperatives and feel no sense of obligation to their employees. Warren Bennis says that corporate CEOs are no longer corporate statesman. He writes: "Today, they have no interest in anything but their own bottom lines. The visionaries, too, are gone. American businessmen never had many moral imperatives, but they did feel some obligation to their employees, the towns they operated in, and the national economy."[15]

Clergy as well as lay leaders feel the pressure to increase giving and membership by a variety of techniques and strategies. This pressure to succeed can lead to a model of leadership overly focused on techniques and numbers – the proverbial "bottom line." Certainly there is a need to attend to the finances and budgets, but that is not the sole mission of the church.

Those clergy who fail at meeting budgets or attending to the "bottom line" turn to denominational officials only to feel a sense of disconnection. One area that reveals the disconnected feeling in the Lutheran denomination is among first-call clergy. A study conducted in the fall of 2002 of first-call ordained pastors of the Evangelical Lutheran Church in America (E.L.C.A.) revealed some disturbing findings. In this study, "The Context for Mission and Ministry in the E.L.C.A.," the greatest dissatisfaction among the 618 respondents was "support from denominational officials."[16] Church critics call it a feeling of disconnection among laity, clergy, and denominational officials.

The resulting decline of mainlines is evident in the membership statistics. From 1990 to 2000 the Lutheran, Presbyterian, Episcopalian, Methodist and United Church of Christ denominations lost a combined total of 1,215,723 members.[17] This decline occurred at a time when the U.S. population was growing. Specifically, while the total membership of all Lutherans, including the Lutheran Church Missouri Synod and The Wisconsin Synod, numbers over seven million in the United States, the church has not grown in proportion to the population. Membership in the Evangelical Lutheran Church in America congregations has not kept pace with the U.S. population.[18] Membership for the years 1998 – 2004 showed steady decline. The figures for the baptized membership per year are as follows; 1998 – 5,178,225, 1999 – 5,149,668, 2000 – 5,125,919, 2001 – 5,099,877, 2002 – 5,038,066, 2003 – 4,984,925, 2004 – 4,930,429.[19]

Kenneth Innskeep, replying to an interview in The Lutheran, says that Lutherans are going to struggle and get by, but that many of our congregations are in locations where businesses are leaving and are not coming back. Young people are leaving the small rural communities and leaving a vacuum of young people. This is particularly true for the congregations in agricultural communities. He notes that the smaller congregations will suffer the most. He writes: "As a result, we have large numbers of small congregations that spend more than they can afford to keep their doors open and pay a pastor."[20]

This decline has serious consequences for congregations of all denominations. The Lutheran denomination is not the only one that could cite the above quotation. While there are thriving congregations throughout the United States, there are just as many in survival mode.

Since a number of mainline denominations have suffered losses, some deduce that members in these congregations are not growing spiritually. Commenting on a perceived lack of spiritual growth among congregations, Michael Foss advocates that churches move from a membership model to a discipleship model.[21]

In the membership model the pastor takes care of all the members and is responsible for their spiritual growth. This is, of course, a flawed model when taken to its logical conclusion. As a congregation grows there will be a point at which the pastor can no longer shepherd the flock effectively. Some church consultants have suggested that a congregation needs one pastor for every one hundred and fifty to two hundred persons in worship.

In the discipleship model the pastor acts as the chief leader to "equip the saints."[22] Everyone has gifts of shepherding and leading. God gives congregations the talent and people needed and it is the clergy and church leaders' job to equip everyone for service.

Whether it be discipleship or another model, the need to take a fresh look at leadership is great. Whatever the reasons for decline--a weak theological base, Herb Miller's theories of feeling spirituality, or consumerist religion--the decline must stop.

Decline must stop not because of a sole need to reverse the waning numbers, though that is important, but out of love for the church. It is the body of Christ and deserves our love and support. The first step in addressing problems is a proper diagnosis; there is a lack of leadership training. The need is great for Christian leadership training, Christian leadership curriculum and Christian leadership renewal for laity and clergy alike. The Fifth Frame is one way to teach Christian leadership while at the same time educating Christian leaders about the fundamentals of the faith.

This book is the explanation of the Fifth Frame, a model of leadership grounded in the orthodox faith of Christianity. These pages offer a model, provide a tool for retreats and seminars, and engage the Christian leader with concepts and characteristics of leadership. Encouragement to press on comes from the words of Jeremiah chapter 1 verse 17, "But you, gird up your loins; stand up and tell them everything that I command you. Do not break down before them or I will break you before them." Read on, interact, critique, enjoy, learn, and most importantly lead!

Introduction: Questions for Reflection

1. If indeed, it is true as Herb Miller writes, "Leadership is not everything in growing a congregation, but it is the something without which little else happens," do you see opportunities for leadership training in your congregation?

2. What does Ephesians 4:11-16 mean to you and how might these words be informative for leaders in your congregation?

3. How would you define Christian leadership?

4. Read Mark 10:42-45. What does this say about leadership?

5. Read 1 Peter 2:1-5. Is your congregation growing, stable, or declining in membership? Are your members growing and longing for "the pure spiritual milk"?

6. Does your congregation have high expectations of its members?

7. Read John 10:16. How might your congregation create a culture of cooperation and dialogue with other Christian congregations in your locale?

8. How might your congregation transform into a community of disciples and reject a consumerist model of ministry?

Chapter One

What is Christian Leadership?

The primary issue to be considered is the question of Christian leadership. John W. Gardner defines leadership in this way: "Leadership is a process of persuasion or example by which an individual (or leadership team) induces a group to pursue objectives held by the leader or shared by the leader and his or her followers."[23] Warren Bennis and Burt Nanus argue that leadership is essential for organizational success. They contend that leadership is the pivotal force for organizations and that leadership is necessary to create a new vision.[24] Change cannot happen without effective leadership.

Many organizations in the United States provide examples of effective leadership. While a number stand out for their effectiveness, Wal – Mart[25] and General Electric are exemplary in leadership, profit, training, and global outreach. Both businesses owe much of their success to a single effective leader.

Wal – Mart has acquired tremendous success. This company was the brainchild of Sam Walton, the founder and visionary leader of the company. He defined "leadership" in ten principles. His rules were commit to your business, share your profits with associates, motivate the partners, communicate, appreciate the associates, celebrate your successes, listen to everyone in your company, exceed your customer's expectations, control your expenses, and ignore the conventional wisdom.[26] He, like other great business leaders, was the strong central leader of the company and the key to its effectiveness.

Leaders not only lead; they also train others to be leaders. Hiring and training leaders was a primary task of Jack Welch at General Electric. Welch is reportedly one of the greatest business leaders in the last two decades. He led General Electric to be a major conglomerate and profit machine. Over a period of thirty years he hired leaders to strengthen General Electric. His rules for leadership were based on four essential traits: leaders must have energy, be able to energize others, have an edge – the courage to make tough decisions, and be able to execute. He asserted that these four traits were ineffective without integrity and intelligence. [27]

Effective organizations are dependent upon competent leadership. Warren Bennis recounted his experience at the University of Cincinnati in which the multitude of daily tasks diverted his attention from doing the right thing. Bennis defined doing the right thing through the use of four competencies of leadership. Competent leaders manage attention, manage meaning, manage trust, and manage self. He argues, as do others, that we do not train people to be leaders. He writes, "Part of our fault lies with our schools of management; we teach people how to be good technicians and good staff people, but we don't train people for leadership."[28]

Since leadership is a pivotal force behind successful organizations, decline in membership and giving to Christian churches can be understood in light of current models of leadership training. A new vision for the church requires an improved commitment to partnerships with state and national offices, a dedication to the mission of the church, a renewed emphasis on equipping the saints to grow in faith and evangelize, and a transformative and comprehensive leadership development and training program.

How can Christian churches strengthen leadership? In the study, "Context for Mission and Ministry in the Evangelical Lutheran Church in America," 824 clergy were surveyed with 618 responding for a return rate of 75%; these were the most recently ordained clergy, those in their first three years of ordained ministry. One question asked about preparation for congregational work. Ratings on this instrument ranged from 1- (not at all prepared) to 5- (very well prepared). The lowest scores were planning a church budget (2.34), planning a stewardship program (2.46), managing a church office (2.99), and managing disputes and conflict situations (3.09). First - call clergy saw, "reaching out to unchurched persons," as the highest need and "helping congregations work toward a vision," as the second highest need.[29] These four activities at the bottom of the list and the need to reach unchurched persons and work toward vision are specific areas that must be targeted for leadership development. Other activities such as preaching, planning a worship service, and visiting members are also relevant to leadership but receive effective attention in seminary training.[30]

This study asked, "At present, what is your level of satisfaction with the following?" Surprisingly, this group of Lutheran clergy rated their "overall effectiveness as a pastoral leader," in this way. Very satisfied- 43%, and somewhat satisfied –51%. This totals to a 94% satisfaction with their effectiveness.[31] But these responses begged the question. Was their satisfaction with their effectiveness misplaced especially in view of their own acknowledged unmet critical needs?

The need to improve leadership training is also a result of the tendency for clergy and lay leaders to oversimplify the church and its structures. Avery Dulles highlighted the various models of the church including the church as the body of Christ, but also stated that the church has an institutional side.[32] As such the church is prone to problems inherent in secular institutions like miscommunication, misinterpretation of communication, morale of employees and parishioners, and financial pressures, to name but a few. The modern church is a complicated organization just as are secular organizations. Lee Bolman and Terrence Deal write:

> But we all know the darker side to organizations. They often frustrate and sometimes exploit the people who work in them. Too often, their products do not work,

their students learn very little, their patients remain ill, and their policies make things worse instead of better.[33]

This can be paraphrased for the church: But we all know the darker side of congregations. They often frustrate and sometimes exploit both the clergy and the laity who work in them. Too often their plans fail, their students do not learn the scripture, their members are spiritually ill and lack depth in discipleship, and their policies make things worse instead of better.

The image of corporations and other organizations is often colored by people's expectations of a simplified structure. It is, after all, through organizations that workers accomplish great tasks. Though organizational life is where many people spend much of their days they are often unaware of the day to day dynamics.

Each year I receive various annual reports from the companies whose stock I own. The reports portray the advertising slogans, colorful pictures, and vision and mission statements. What we do not see is the complexity and confusion that often abound. There is both beauty and beast in organizational life.

Organizations have a number of distinct properties that contribute to their complexity. These include surprise, deceptiveness, and ambiguity. Organizations can be surprising due to the inability to predict the outcome of decisions or initiatives. Organizations can be deceptive due to fear of reprimand by those in senior positions. The ambiguity of organizations includes a list highlighted by Bolman and Deal. The list includes seven potential places of ambiguity. These are, we are not sure what the problem is, we are not sure what is really happening, we are not sure what we want, we do not have the resources we need, we are not sure who is supposed to do what, we are not sure how to get what we want, and we are not sure how to determine if we have succeeded.[34]

Congregational life is often filled with surprise. While plans are often made, the execution of those plans can falter or be changed when implemented. Congregations are surprised when a policy put in place to help control use of church facilities and share expenses with those who use the facilities causes hurt feelings among families. Churches are surprised when pre-marriage preparation policies put in place to help young couples prepare for marriage are viewed as a hurdle to overcome. Parishes are surprised when plans are made and put aside only to come to fruition years later, no doubt attributable to God's great timing.

Ambiguities abound in congregations. Congregations often have to deal with the ambiguity of the availability of funds. Roles are sometimes unclear and there is often overlap of responsibilities. Laity often do not have specific job descriptions in congregations and, as such, there is duplication and/or confusion over who is to do what.

Information shared through newsletters, bulletins, and verbal announcements is often repeated frequently. It is however, often unheard or, even worse, misinterpreted.

For example, one congregation had a staff member resign for personal reasons. This was reported to the congregation by letter. Due to the miniscule information given, rumors abounded. Members filled the void with false information such as he was fired and that he left because of health complications.

The complexity, ambiguity, and overall difficulty in leadership in church organizations is due in part not only to oversimplification of its structure but also to mental models brought to the leadership task. According to Peter Senge, "mental models are deeply ingrained assumptions, generalizations, or even pictures or images that influence how we understand the world and how we take action."[35] Clergy and key lay leaders bring various mental models to the leadership task. One false assumption about congregations that is often held by pastors and others is that churches are completely harmonious groups of people. Once I passed a church with the following words emblazoned over the front entrance, "The Perfect Church."

Stunned, I pointed this out to my twin sons who had to endure a mini-sermon on the error of such a statement. Douglas John Hall wrote that there is no perfect church, only the perfect love of God.[36]

Conflict in the church is often shunned, downplayed, ignored, or even presumed to not exist. Scriptural records indicate that the early church wrestled with complicated issues that caused conflict. In Galatians chapter 2, Paul confronted Peter in front of the crowd because he drew back from eating with Gentiles. In Acts 15, an argument erupted over the issue of circumcision and a council was held to decide the outcome. The church at Corinth was plagued by divisions as well as moral and ethical disorders.

The reformers of the church in the Middle Ages knew full well the extent of conflict in the church. In the Apology to the Augsburg Confession, a Lutheran confessional document, Philip Melanchthon wrote:

> If the church, which is truly the kingdom of Christ, is distinguished from the kingdom of the devil, it necessarily follows that since the wicked belong to the kingdom of the devil, they are not the church. In this life, nevertheless, because the kingdom of Christ has not yet been revealed, they are mingled with the church and hold office in the church.[37]

How many of you have entertained the notion that those who belong to the kingdom of the devil hold office in the church? While it may offend our sensibilities, let us not be so naïve. The devil and his legions of demons conduct his major battles in the midst of our congregations. Put another way, Pastor Mark Chavez writes, "If we could build a spiritual reconnaissance satellite with infrared sensors that detect 'hot,' destructive opposition to the work of the Holy Spirit, the hottest spots on the satellite images would be in the churches."[38] The source of the conflict is sin. This is but one of the generalizations many leaders hold about the church.

There are many assumptions and generalizations of the church that can be linked to faulty mental models. For instance each member represents the values and commitment of the entire congregation. Also pastors are responsible for caring for every member and enabling them to grow spiritually. Another model may be that a congregational vote or a consensus means that an issue is completely settled. And most disputed: the church should never ask for money or the church should always ask for money.

These assumptions and generalizations plus many others determine how leaders take action. For instance, a prevailing thought among some church leaders and consultants is that congregations grow numerically with a contemporary worship service. This would be only one part of a complicated effort to reach unchurched persons and would be an oversimplification. Peter Senge calls this a leap of abstraction.[39] The leader moves from direct observation – the congregation is not growing – to generalization without testing – the congregation must add a contemporary worship service, or abolish a traditional service and adopt only a contemporary style.[40] While congregational growth and effectiveness is the result of an entire system of ministries and plans, leadership is the one central part.

In the task of leadership, clergy and lay leaders bring different and often incomplete mental models for understanding congregations. Clergy and lay leaders who master the skills of reflective listening and care deeply will be surprised and frustrated by the complexities of parish life. While these skills are essential, more is needed. To avoid this frustration and confusion, Bolman and Deal advocate the concept of integrated leadership defined in this way: "Wise leaders understand their own strengths, work to expand them, and build teams that together can provide leadership in all four modes – structural, political, human resource, and symbolic."[41]

This style of leadership brings together four schools of thought: political, structural, symbolic, and human resource frames. Bolman and Deal use the term "frames" because these viewpoints are windows through which leaders view organizations. Each frame provides a different view. Managers and leaders must be skillful at using these frames and learning how to match the frame to the situation.[42] Preparation for parish ministry does not include exposure to this model nor training in a comprehensive biblical model of leadership. The George Barna Research group examined the curriculums of today's seminaries and concluded that they do little to prepare clergy to effectively run an organization and very few provide training in leadership.[43]

Integrated four-frame leadership as proposed by Bolman and Deal, while comprehensive and effective for secular leaders, lacks a spiritual component. This presents a serious dilemma for lay and clergy leaders. In my research pastors found the concepts very helpful, but they also indicated a need for a spiritual basis for leadership. No one, however, could articulate just what that model should look like.

While visiting my mother and away from the usual church distractions, I sat in her living room doodling on a legal pad. Almost as quickly as a flash of light, my doodling turned into a diagram capturing various components of leadership. I call it the Fifth Frame.

This Fifth Frame is a comprehensive biblical model of leadership. This model integrates biblical leadership with the theological concepts of being, becoming, and doing. For those who are visual learners, this model and the accompanying diagram will prove very useful not only for clergy but also for every Christian whom God calls to lead. The model is the combination not only of numerous models regarding leadership as well as a study of the biblical text, but also an abundance of prayer and thought. While there are many problems in the contemporary church, this book addresses the need for distinctly Christian leadership. Read on as God calls you to greater depths of leadership.

Chapter One: Questions for Reflection

1. Is there a Christian leader who mentored you?
2. Have you experienced miscommunications in your congregation? Read Colossians 1:3-6. Could your congregation intentionally focus on spreading faith in Jesus Christ in every meeting?
3. Does your congregation have descriptions of its ministries and the spiritual gifts needed for them? Read and reflect on 1 Corinthians 12:28
4. If there is no "perfect church," how would you describe your congregation?
5. Has your congregation experienced conflict? If so, how did you handle it? Read and reflect on, 1 Corinthians 2: 1-5. Is our faith resting on human wisdom and not the power of God when we are embroiled in conflict?
6. A "leap of abstraction," is moving from direct observation – the congregation is not growing – to generalization without testing. Has your congregation made this error in judgment before? If so, how has the leadership learned from it?
7. Is your congregation currently involved in leadership training of any kind?

Chapter Two

Toward a Curriculum of Leadership

One fundamental premise of Christian leadership is that God equips those whom God calls. Does this mean that training or education is unnecessary? Certainly not! There are some that might contend otherwise. One of the itinerant preachers of the early 1800's was Peter Cartwright who held disdain for the education of clergy. He wrote: "Now this educated ministry and theological training are no longer an experiment. Other denominations have tried them, and they have proved a perfect failure."[44] It is unconscionable that someone would hold education for clergy or any other lay leader with such contempt. Clearly, the Reverend Cartwright had strong views about education and its power to corrupt. Sadly, many feel that the call of a church leader needs no verification or formal training.

It is, however, incumbent upon all Christians to grow in knowledge and skills. In 2 Peter chapter one scripture encourages us to continue our growth in knowledge. Saint Peter writes,

> For this very reason, you must make every effort to support your faith with goodness, and goodness with knowledge...For if these things are yours and are increasing among you, they keep you from being ineffective and unfruitful in the knowledge of our Lord Jesus Christ.[45]

Clergy and lay leaders are called to grow in their knowledge. Peter writes that the knowledge is to increase so that the leader does not become ineffective. One way leaders grow and learn is by equipping others for service in God's church. Just what does it mean to equip?

The second parish I served, Faith Lutheran in Batesburg, South Carolina, initiated a capital fund campaign. When the need for renovation and an addition to the building was identified, my first task as pastor was to recruit someone for the task of fund raising. Did I as Pastor need to know everything regarding a capital fund campaign? Of course not! I recruited Charlie Miller, a retired Brigadier General. Charlie had the skills, knowledge, expertise, and leadership necessary to effectively rally the congregation and create a capital campaign. He created a slogan, "Operation Nehemiah," based on the biblical story of building the walls of Jerusalem. As I interacted with him and supported him as Pastor, I learned much about how to inspire and run a capital campaign.

Equipping does not imply that we give people the tools and knowledge they need for the task. Even though Paul instructs us to "equip the saints,"[46] this does not imply that Christian leaders need to know everything. Rather the leader equips through the Word of God and prayer. As the Reverend Dr. Dearld Sterling, a Baptist clergy friend of mine so succinctly said, "God gives a congregation the leaders it needs to do the ministry God calls them to do."

Continuing education for clergy and lay leaders is not an opportunity to acquire another certificate to hang on our wall, but rather a chance to confront closely held truths and renew our sense of mission. Elders, boards, or deacons could work as a team along with clergy to discern what gifts and skills are most needed for their congregation. Does the congregation need the gift of persuasion, compassion or even a shrewd negotiator?

For the past seven years I have met weekly with a Presbyterian minister. We pray, eat breakfast, fellowship, and prepare talking points for our respective sermons. One morning a man approached our table and asked, "Are you studying the

Bible?" "Why, yes we are," we replied. Then the unexplainable happened. He explained that we were not supposed to use our minds to study the scripture. I was aghast at his sincere dismay that we were studying the scripture. His reasoning went something like this: all we need to know is right there and we do not need to study it because it is simple and in plain view.

Continuing training and education opens our hearts and minds to new thought and new insight. We truly can learn from other caring Christians. One pastor with whom I conducted a funeral told me of his call to ministry. Upon further discussion I discovered that he had no college, seminary, or individual training for ordained ministry. This lack of formal education means that he had never been challenged about his training or practice of ministry. He then informed me that the congregation he founded had a board of elders he chose. When I asked how the board was organized he replied, "They do what I tell them, and if they disagree with me I remove them from my board."[47] Does this style of leadership help anyone grow and learn?

God's call invites the believer to deepen one's spiritual relationship. God's desire for the aspiring leader is that he has a heart open to transformation. Note that God loved King David because he had "a heart for God." From this loving passion to know God flows a desire for leadership development and education.

Clearly, education can be an effective means to develop clergy and lay people in their ability to think and lead with the Fifth Frame model. Training in the Fifth Frame can be done through a comprehensive curriculum of leadership. The assumption that leaders are born, not made, is false.

I believe that leadership development begins not with an understanding of the various models and theories of leadership, but it begins with God. The ability to improve a Christian leader's skill, intuition, and practice of leadership can be done with an explicit grounding in the Fifth Frame model which incorporates several concepts and leadership models into a comprehensive biblical model.

What happens when there is a lack of leadership? In practice, the result of an incomplete mental model of leadership too often leads to failure. Consider the results shared by one clergy of a weekend retreat in which the elected leaders sought to restructure and simplify the church organization. The retreat setting enabled all the leaders to share openly and express their desires for a renewed mission. Worship, prayer, singing, and inspiration marked the retreat. An entire structure was devised only to die in committee upon return to the parish.

The elected leaders in retreat viewed the task from a human resource perspective with lots of participation and sharing. They listened to each other's concerns and supported each other. A telling comment by one parishioner not in attendance at the retreat underscored the failure of restructuring: "Too few people will have too much influence." Concern and sensitivity for this person's feelings would not have changed anything or accomplished the defined goal of restructuring the committees. The comment betrayed the parishioner's concern for power while the elected leaders were concerned with the participation of each elected leader. In this situation, political skills were needed in addition to careful listening and oversight of the organizational dynamics. The use of the Fifth Frame of biblical leadership can prevent such well-meaning plans from going awry.

The quality of leadership can be improved with the Fifth Frame as a foundational model. We make this claim because of the impact of the four frame approach to leadership first described by Bolman and Deal. The Fifth Frame is the Christian perspective intermingled with their work. Their work, and the work of others who utilized their leadership inventory, provides an excellent baseline for analysis of leadership styles and behaviors.

In order to develop an effective training program, a preliminary assessment of current needs and leadership behaviors must be made. From 1997 to 1999, I conducted an extensive analysis of clergy of the Lutheran denomination in the state of South Carolina using an instrument that measured leadership styles as defined by Lee Bolman and Terrence Deal. More than 125 clergy and 55 lay persons participated in the study. A smaller focus group of nine clergy participated in non-directed interviews about leadership specifically with the four frames. The data generated from these nine and the larger group, though a relatively small universe, provided substantial insight in the leadership behaviors of this select group. The data from the study demonstrated that pastors chose human resource behaviors most often. [48]

What best describes a human resource leader? The human resource leader views organizations as primarily composed of individuals who have needs, feelings, and prejudices. The key to effectiveness in the view of the human resource frame is for an organization to be centered on the strengths of the people. It is "to find an organizational form that enables people to get the job done while feeling good about what they are doing."[49]

The Pastoral leader who uses the human resource frame most often is one who is supportive, encouraging, and helpful. Charles Somervill explains this as "An Identification Strategy."[50] In this leadership approach people follow the pastoral leader because they identify with him. They identify with the pastoral leader because he knows their needs, listens to them, and is available.

Note, however, that the exclusive use of human resource behaviors without the Christian core is detrimental to clergy leadership. The sole use of this frame hinders the casting of a congregational vision and is ineffective when necessary to implement new ministries. At its extreme, a human resource leader would lead by opinions, whims, and wishes of the congregation.

The clergy in our focus group utilized human resource leadership models most often. While there is nothing inherently wrong with this style, other perspectives are necessary. Clergy and lay leaders need to see leadership from a broader perspective. Educational models begin with current realities and attempt to stretch or broaden one's perceptions. An educational curriculum based on Fifth Frame principles could offer such a perspective.

An instructional leadership program has many different components. According to Decker Walker and Jonas Soltis, "By far the most influential set of ideas about how to make a curriculum is embodied in the 'Tyler Rationale.'"[51] Tyler organized his thoughts around four fundamental questions, which he claims are central to developing any curriculum: 1. What educational purposes should the school seek to attain? 2. What educational experiences can be provided that are likely to attain these purposes? 3. How can these educational experiences be effectively organized? 4. How can we determine whether these purposes are being attained? [52]

Daniel Tanner and Laurel Tanner observe that Tyler's questions represent a four – step sequence of 1. Identifying objectives 2. Selecting the means for the attainment of these objectives 3. Organizing these means, and 4. Evaluating the outcomes. [53] In their book on curriculum development, the authors developed a more satisfactory paradigm in their curriculum report on Tyler's Eight-Year Study. Their paradigm for curriculum development illustrates the four problem areas as interdependent functions rather than as linear steps.

George J. Posner and Alan N. Rudnitsky offer a different model for curriculum design. It begins with values and through a specific process moves to educational goals, curriculum, instructional plan, actual learning outcome, educational results and evaluation. They warn that this is not a linear procedural flowchart. They write: "Therefore it is important when using this framework to remember that it is a conceptual overview rather than a procedural flowchart of the course design process." [54]

Using this framework, the core value or philosophy for a leadership-training program would be the Fifth Frame. Goals could include enabling clergy or lay leaders to articulate their relationship with God in Christ, their sense of call to leadership, their further discernment of gifts to lead, their primary biblical leadership characteristics, and to enable them to think about leadership with political, structural, human resource, and symbolic categories.

My study used a non-directive structured interview process to encourage thinking with the four frames and theological reflection. Other possibilities for a basic curriculum design could include the case study method, a proven method for education of clergy and an approach used by Bolman and Deal.[55] The plan could include review, discussion and analysis of a case. The actual learning outcome could be the ability for the clergy or lay leader to articulate organizational processes such as goal setting, decision making, planning etc. from the perspective of the Fifth Frame model. An excellent tool for analysis of the organizational processes is given in the text *Reframing Organizations*.[56] Evaluation of each step could provide necessary modifications throughout the process.

An integrated leadership training and development program and focus on the Fifth Frame would be one major step to reverse the decline in membership. Leaders trained in this model could assist in removing the distrust at all levels and work through, or at the least, significantly reduce congregational conflicts. Leaders using the Fifth Frame model and various tools can exercise effectively their God given talents in strengthening the local congregation, all for the glory of God.

Chapter Two: Questions for Reflection

1. Have you done continuing education in the past year? Is your congregational leadership team committed to regular learning?
2. How do your congregational leaders equip others to do ministry?
3. Does your congregational leaders allow for diversity of opinions?
4. How might the Fifth Frame enable your leadership to deal constructively with conflict?
5. Study the "Fifth Frame" diagram. How might you use it to strengthen leadership in your congregation?
6. Read and reflect on Ephesians 4:15-16.

Chapter Three

What is The Core of Christian Leadership?
"Being"

The central characteristic of Christian leadership is a relationship with God in Jesus Christ. Theological training must root the student firmly in relationship with Jesus Christ. While there are essentials to know in leading such as structures, finances, policies, and systems, salvation in Christ is the foundation. We cannot become overly focused on the practice of leadership and its attendant traits. The 103rd Archbishop of Canterbury expressed it this way: "Otherwise the whiz-kids we may create – while knowing all about information technology and all the specialisms of ministry – may have little to offer the faith –needs of our world; or yours."[57] While structures, management, policy, and finances are important parts of the church organizational puzzle, not one of them is the key piece.

This chapter sets forth the theological and biblical foundations for Christian leadership and illustrates the first component of a comprehensive model of leadership. The whole model incorporates literature on leadership regarding characteristics, behaviors, and the centrality of God. The name given to the entire model of biblical leadership is the Fifth Frame. The components of the model include God's transcendence, the Word of God, wisdom, the call of God, discipleship, discernment, humility, and primary biblical leadership characteristics and behaviors. Practical examples of leadership are given with Moses and Jesus as well as examples from other pastoral leaders.

Teaching Christian leadership is more than learning a set of behaviors or a way of thinking. While embracing modern methods and models of leadership can be fruitful, Christian leadership primarily serves the proclamation of the gospel. Scott Hendrix notes that ministers must know something about organizational management in order that the gospel might be communicated effectively.[58]

Leadership for Christians is a feedback loop. The behaviors are related to the core characteristics that in turn flow from a relationship with God and exist for the sake of the gospel. The task of educating Christians to be better leaders requires an awareness and articulation of God's call. A leadership development model, therefore, must include reflection on the transcendence and power of God. Clearly, God directs and guides those whom he calls.

A sole focus on leadership techniques without including God in the equation automatically results in a flawed approach to leadership in church organizations and maybe even in secular organizations. The heart of the Christian leader is a heart for God and the heart of leadership is God. The most precious gift to Christian leaders is the Holy Spirit.

In the first chapter of Acts, Jesus tells us that we will receive power when the Holy Spirit comes. Do Christian leaders anchor themselves in this power? Make no mistake; it is not "the force" as depicted in the famous science fiction drama *Star Wars*. Rather, the Holy Spirit brings the leader power to communicate the Word of God. The preacher delivers the Word from the pulpit but all Christian leaders proclaim the Word.

In the book of Acts, chapter 2, Luke describes with captivating language the arrival of the Holy Spirit. Peter speaks to the crowd and concludes with these words, "Therefore let the entire house of Israel know with certainty that God has made him both Lord and Messiah, this Jesus whom you crucified."[59]

This is our message of power; the power of God to destroy death to all who will believe. Thus, there is more to leadership and more to education than an exercise in intellectual stimulation.

John Leith argues there is a crisis in theological education. This crisis is rooted in an attempt to accommodate the theology of the church to the culture. He argues that post enlightenment theologians such as Schleiermacher gave too little emphasis to the fundamentals of the faith while writing theology.[60] He cites the work of James Turner who wrote, "Put slightly differently, unbelief emerged because church leaders too often forgot the transcendence essential to any worthwhile God."[61] Christian leadership emerges from a transcendent and holy God.

Leith submits that the decline in seminary education is also a result of an overemphasis on parochial causes, and the teaching of the seminary that inculcates academics rather than faith. He notes that seminaries should not assume the functions of a secular university with a critical reflection on the faith, but rather focus on the proclaiming and transmission of the faith.[62] The transmission of the faith and the education of Christian leaders are rooted in their relationships with God. Leadership development for Christians begins with an understanding of the majesty, omniscience, omnipresence, and omnipotence of God. In essence, Christian leadership has a dimension that is over and above the skills and behaviors of the secular leader.

This wholly other dimension is biblical integrated leadership, the Fifth Frame, an inclusive paradigm of leadership centered in one's relationship with God.

The core of the Fifth Frame is God. Lay leaders and clergy alike must acknowledge God as transcendent, as defined in scripture. George Buttrick writes that Revelation is "God's unveiling or uncovering of himself and his purposes."[63] An ancient hymn expresses God's transcendence this way, "Immortal, invisible, God only wise, in light inaccessible hid from our eyes."[64]

God is infinite and source of all wisdom. God is, therefore, the source of all wisdom and purposeful leadership. Several contemporary songs capture the meaning of transcendence with their emphasis on humility and reverence. For instance the song, "God Forbid," by Point of Grace, underscores our need to speak with God with a humble reverence in our hearts and not speak to God in an all too familiar way.

God's transcendence prods us to pray with a humble reverence in our heart. In God's transcendence God chooses to uncover himself that we might be transformed. Reinhold Niebuhr understood God's transcendence as that which enables human beings to confront the evil that resides in us. Only in that confrontation can human beings truly know themselves.

Another expression of God's transcendence is God's holiness. George Buttrick writes about holiness in his interpretation of the book of Isaiah, "Holiness is not just the measure of the infinite gulf between the sublimity of God and the creatureliness of man; it is the awesome contrast between God's purity and man's sin."[65] It is God's holiness and transcendence that makes leaders aware of their total dependence on God. God's transcendence puts us in our place and makes the leader aware that he or she is not at the center of all that happens or does not happen in a congregation.

God called Moses through supernatural means. As Moses stood before the burning bush, God said, "Do not come near here; remove your sandals from your feet, for the place on which you are standing is holy ground."[66] The holiness of God elicited fear and Moses hid his face. Jeffrey Niehaus writes: "On one hand, it may be that Yahweh does not want Moses to be entirely unafraid; Moses must understand that he is in the presence of a holy God."[67] The fear and reverence of God is the beginning of wisdom. The theophany, a manifestation of God, does not serve merely to elicit fear in Moses, but rather is God's way of communicating his holy presence. Niehaus continues: "Theophanic radiance and power communicate to the natural senses what it means thus purely *to be*."[68]

Although a huge gulf exists between the purity of God and the frailty of human beings, God's transcendence draws the believer into relationship. Terence E. Fretheim writes: "The divine holiness is of such a character that it invites rather than repels human response, inviting Moses into genuine conversation."[69]

The center of the Fifth Frame model of leadership is the transcendent God and not the leader nor the skills of leadership. This model of leadership emanates from God who has all wisdom. Note that wisdom is included in the concentric circle with the Word of God. It is this wisdom that guides and directs God's people. Any Christian model that places leaders and their skills in the center simply misses the mark as it fails to acknowledge God's transcendence and might.

What we know about God is revealed in God's written Word. The scripture is the next concentric circle in the Fifth Frame leadership model.

The written Word of God is central to the life of the church. It is however, the interpretation of scripture that elicits the most consternation among believers. There are a variety of views on scripture from the positions known as verbal inspiration or literalism to those who hold that the scripture is a culturally bound book alongside other classics of literature. This continuum of views is no solace to those who seek to understand the scripture but rather is a continuing source of contention. Labels are attached to those on either side of the spectrum such as liberal or conservative. Often those labels are used exclusively as the only way to define one Christian as opposed to another. These labels do not advance dialogue and understanding among believers.

With a measure of hilarity, I know that some view the Bible itself as a symbol of an unwanted fundamentalism. When the pastor of Harvard, Peter Gomes, was offered pew bibles many questions ensued. Foremost of those questions was "What does the benefactor want or expect?" Some warned Gomes "people will think that this is a fundamentalist church. If they see bibles in the pews, you will have an image problem."[70] What are we to do and where are we to go in this maze of views? While there are a variety of views, there is a lot of common ground. Note the following doctrinal positions on scripture. Noted Baptist historian Robert G. Torbet wrote:

Baptists, to a greater degree than any other group, have strengthened the protest of evangelical Protestantism against traditionalism. This they have done by their constant witness to the supremacy of the Scriptures as the all-sufficient and sole norm for faith and practice in the Christian life.[71]

The Westminster Confession of Faith has ten tenets; Tenet four states:

The authority of the Holy Scripture, for which it ought to be believed, and obeyed, dependeth not upon the testimony of any man, or Church; but wholly upon God (who is truth itself) the author thereof; and therefore it is to be received, because it is the Word of God.[72]

The Methodist Church in its *Book of Discipline* states:

United Methodists share with other Christians the conviction that Scripture is the primary source and criterion for Christian doctrine. Through Scripture the living Christ meets us in the experience of redeeming grace. We are convinced that Jesus Christ is the living Word of God in our midst whom we trust in life and death.[73]

My own denomination elaborates on its doctrine of the scripture in the constitution as well as in the confessional writings. The written Word reveals the living Word. The constitution of the E.L.C.A. states that the scriptures are centered in the revelation of Jesus Christ:

The canonical Scriptures of the Old and New Testaments are the written Word of God. Inspired by God's Spirit speaking through their authors, they record and announce God's revelation centering in

Jesus Christ. Through them God's Spirit speaks to us to create and sustain Christian faith and fellowship for service in the world.[74]

The confessional teachings of the Lutheran church state: We believe, teach, and confess that the prophetic and apostolic writings of the Old and New Testaments are the only rule and norm according to which all doctrines and teachers alike must be appraised and judged, as it is written in Psalm 119:105, "Thy Word is a lamp to my feet and a light to my path."[75]

The official doctrines of the various churches while they hold much in common also reflect the diverse views of those in the pews. Consider this conversation. While working in a store, a shopper inquired about a book with a curious cover. The shop clerk, a Christian, told him that the book was actually a Bible. The shopper said, "Oh, I don't believe the Bible, but I believe in Jesus." To which the storeowner inquired, "You believe in Jesus, but not the Bible?"[76] This surprising exchange is puzzling at best for the question's it raises. What do individuals believe about the bible? While there are a variety of opinions, the clearest is that the Holy Scripture reveals Christ.

From the denominational statements above one can assert that scripture is the source of our doctrine and the guide for our lives in Jesus Christ. It is important to note that for many scholars the Word of God is more than that which is written. Karl Barth spoke of the preeminent Word in Jesus Christ, the account of the Word in the bible, and the proclamation of the Word in preaching. The primary note to sound is that the Word of God is a living Word. Much more could be said, of course, but as I am not attempting a systematic theology of the Word, this will have to suffice. With the Holy Spirit, God breathes through the scriptures and enlightens and equips Christians to be leaders. What we learn from scripture is God initiates relationships and that God has an overwhelming love for his people. This is clearly articulated in a doctrine of the Word by Joseph Sittler. He wrote: "The content of that address was that God, to whom he could not rise, had come to him; that the righteousness of God which he could not satisfy had been bestowed; that genuine freedom was a gift of God, and that in Jesus Christ that gift was proffered out of the initiative, the measureless and the shocking love of God."[77]

The Holy Scripture is "God's Word. All of it is useful for teaching and helping people and for correcting them and showing them how to live."[78] The Word strengthens and directs the believer and leader in growth and service. The Word is an irresistible force because it emanates from the holy and transcendent God.

As Isaiah prophesied, "so shall my Word be that goes forth from my mouth; it shall not return to me empty, but it shall accomplish that which I purpose, and prosper in the thing for which I sent it."[79] The Word of God accomplishes all things through the leader. Luther wrote, "So our building and promotion of the church is not the result of our works but of the Word of God which we preach. Here you see that everything is produced by the Word."[80]

At the Sumter Ministerial Association, The Reverend Michael Baynai, a Presbyterian minister, shared a helpful insight from his sabbatical. He said that in his entire ordained ministry he worked hard because he wanted God to love him more. He said that God spoke to him in a season of prayer saying, "Son, I cannot love you more, I love you completely." What we need to hear is that the Word of God will prosper in that for which God sends it. This means that the leader's job is not a frantic fire-dousing at every conflict and congregational issue. It is rather the leader's job to trust God and hold up the Word of God before the people in all times.

The Reverend Frank Honeycutt wrote about a project in which he solicited comments' on sermons from skeptics and seekers. Honeycutt reiterates the promise of God's Word that it shall not return empty. He writes, "Therefore, one primary task of preaching is to help others see scripture not as holding rabbit's-foot power (we've all played "Bible Ouija" and sought guidance with a random finger) but rather redeeming power."[81] God's Word redeems us through the power of Jesus

Christ. God's Word forms the Christian leader and imparts God's will. Hans Schwarz writes, "God's Word is accusing and condemning as well as promising and freeing. Yet in both cases it is an active and powerful Word. It affects the life of the people and communicates God's will."[82] God uses his Word to form his leaders and direct his leaders to shape the Christian community.

While I was in seminary, Dr. J.B. Bedenbaugh, professor of New Testament and now in the Church Triumphant, would occasionally utilize video clips to teach. In one class it was clear that Dr. Bedenbaugh wanted us to understand the importance of scripture in the life of a believer. We were watching an interview of Anita Bryant. Some will recall that Mrs. Bryant was an actress and television star. She had been removed from her advertising job because of her vocal expressions of certain moral views. In the interview she was asked, "Have you read the entire Bible?" To which she replied, "No." This was quite a revealing answer. Anyone who aspires to be a leader in the church of Jesus Christ cannot answer "no" to that question. If we are to lead, we must not only know the scripture from our regular reading of it, but we must also allow it to transform us. One could say that the Word equips the leader in every way. Luther wrote that everything depends on the teaching of the word. He wrote: "For we teach with the Word, we consecrate with the Word, we bind and absolve sins by the Word, we baptize with the Word, we sacrifice with the Word, we judge all things by the Word."[83]

Christian leadership is centered in a holy and transcendent God incarnate in Jesus Christ and revealed in the Holy Scripture. The Word of God is the second circle in the Fifth Frame model. There is no Christian leadership without the Word of God.

Flowing from the Word of God is the next concentric circle in the fifth frame model; the call of God.

While attending the funeral of the professor of preaching at Lutheran Theological Southern Seminary, my friend's pager began beeping. Frantically, he tried to shut it off only to resort to removing the batteries. Today, the presence of cellular phones threatens to interrupt the most sacred of moments. We can be called at any time by anyone. Would it not be simple if our call from God were so crystal clear? If only God's voice could ring in our ears and alert us to his call in our life! While it can be stated unequivocally that the call of God always comes to the baptized believer, it is not always so clear.

When I shared my thoughts about ordained ministry with my great uncle he said, "Son, be sure that the GP formation you saw in the clouds as you looked up to the heavens meant 'Go Preach' and not 'Go Plow.'" Undoubtedly, many individuals believe that God issues his call by writing an invitation in the clouds. My great uncle's phrase in a simple comical way communicates a profound truth of the call from God. God's call in our lives should be verifiable. Are there innate gifts that can be cultivated so that one can preach rather than plow? Is there evidence that the one called is open to the Spirit of God moving and directing their life?

The call from God makes Christian leadership distinctly different. In one of our doctoral classes students were asked to articulate their theology of ministry. What was most interesting was how a number of ministers defined their theology by what they do. Christian leadership is more than what we do. Any model of leadership that is overly focused on techniques and behaviors is ineffective if not rooted in the centrality of God. God's call equips and empowers the Christian leader. All Christian leadership is initiated by a call from God. Fretheim reiterates that we do not initiate the call. He writes, "The emphasis throughout is on the divine initiative. It is God who confronts Moses and calls him to a task. Moses does not prepare for the encounter, nor does he seek it. He is surprised by what happens."[84] Each call narrative in Scripture is unique to the individual and yet there are common themes. Christian leadership is no leadership without a call from God.

God called Moses through a burning bush. Moses witnessed the fire but the bush was not consumed. This was symbolic of God's call to lead. God calls Christian leaders and transforms them day by day and experience by experience, but God does not consume them. As H.L. Ellison states, "The flame of fire is the glory of God's presence, which transforms but does not consume." [85] God transforms leaders by his presence.

Moses responds in five ways. Each time Moses offers an excuse. In the final objection Moses says, "Oh, my Lord, send, I pray, some other person."[86] This pattern of hesitancy is seen throughout the biblical narrative. God calls Gideon, "The Lord is with you, you mighty man of valor."[87] Gideon responds by saying that his clan is the weakest in Manasseh and Gideon is the least in his family. God calls Isaiah through a vision in the temple and Isaiah responds, "Woe is me! For I am lost; for I am a man of unclean lips, and I dwell in the midst of a people of unclean lips; for my eyes have seen the King, the Lord of hosts!"[88] God calls the prophet Jeremiah, "Before I formed you in the womb I knew you, and before you were born I consecrated you; I appointed you a prophet to the nations."[89] Jeremiah responds with reservations as do so many others, by saying that he was only a youth and unable to speak. God calls Saul of Tarsus while he was "still breathing threats and murder against the disciples of the Lord."[90] God's call comes without regard to prior qualifications. God does not call the equipped but equips the called.

What does this mean for you the congregational leader? The hesitancy to lead is borne out of fear and a reluctance to yield control of our lives. When I attended a Via De Cristo[91] weekend in 1999 and the leader suggested we remove our watches, I reacted in a rebellious manner and simply refused to abide by the request. A few hours later I consented, realizing that my only reasons were pure rebellion. The effect cultivated in the retreat is to trust the leaders to take care of you and lead you through the weekend. Many of us monitor our watches hourly while we know that God is in control of our day to day activities. As Christian leaders, we trust God to provide guidance and support. This does not mean we have to take off our watches, but it does mean our time is Gods and God is in control and thus can equip us with what we need to do his work.

God often calls some very unlikely candidates. These leaders are not born with all the essential leadership qualities and are often noted for their frailties. Consider Jacob. God called Jacob and yet it was Jacob who secured Esau's birthright by deception. Similarly, God called Moses to go to Egypt and deliver the Hebrews from slavery and yet it was Moses who killed an Egyptian and hid the body in the sand. God set aside the young man David through the prophet Samuel to be king of Israel. David was the youngest of Jesse's sons, the least likely candidate for anointing.

God called seemingly unusual candidates and yet God's call imparted God's authority. Moses objected to God's call on his life and said, "But behold, they will not believe me or listen to my voice, for they will say, 'The Lord did not appear to you.'" [92] God gave Moses a staff and with it Moses demonstrated that God's authority and power was with him.

The leader called by God is equipped with abilities and empowered with authority. The authority, however, is not an inherent trait of the one called, but rather is a gift of God.

Are we open to the "least likely" among us to lead in ministry? Years ago I heard a seminary recruiter tell a congregation, "Send us your brightest and best." Certainly there is need for seminaries to recruit students with high academic standards and those who are best for the job. The phrase, however, troubled me for what it lacked. Perhaps, a better phrasing would be, "Send us the students God is calling!" God calls whomever God calls and not always the person churches think they should call. God may or may not call the captain of the football team for ministry. God may or may not call the most broken person. God calls and the decision is God's.

A friend and colleague shared the story of his summer camp experience with the mentally challenged. During the prayer time one of the mentally challenged campers offered a prayer that ended with, "and God, I am in charge here." The person who is in charge is the person God puts in charge through the power of God's call.

The call of God communicates God's presence. The Israelites followed Moses because they knew that God was with him. They saw him perform mighty miracles strengthening their belief that God was with him such as the incident at the Red Sea. What if you had been sitting on the sea bank on that fateful day? Along comes a train of thousands of people chased by a large powerful army. Suddenly, the people come to the edge of the sea. What will they do? Moses lifted his staff and stretched out his hand over the Red sea and it parted.

In the Hebrew's battle with the Amalekites, Moses stood on top of the hill with the rod of God in his hand. The scripture reports, "Whenever Moses held up his hand, Israel prevailed; and whenever he lowered his hand, Amalek prevailed."[93] The rod held by Moses identified him as God's leader and as one who represented God in the midst of the people.

God calls and God equips, but this does not mean the leader is always effective. King Saul lost his effectiveness and the blessings of God due to disobedience at Gilgal. The prophet Samuel told Saul,

> You have done foolishly; you have not kept the commandment of the Lord your God which he commanded you; for now the Lord would have established your kingdom over Israel forever. But now your kingdom shall not continue; the Lord has sought out a man after his own heart; [94]

Rehoboam sought counsel first from the older men who had advised his father Solomon and then from the younger men. The younger men advised that Rehoboam add even greater burdens to the people. Rehoboam made a poor and politically unwise choice and followed the advice of the younger men. He added greater burdens to the people and eventually this led to the division of the kingdom. [95]

God continues to call leaders for his Church. In the Lutheran Church it is imperative that those who wish to serve as pastoral leaders are extended an official letter of call. This letter is merely an outward sign verifying the inward call. This call by God through the Church for full-time service is specifically reserved for those in the ministry of Word and sacrament and is given for the sake of good order. The confessions state, "It is taught among us that nobody should publicly teach or preach or administer the sacraments in the church without a regular call."[96] While the ordained have a specific action that certifies them as pastoral leaders, how do we endorse the leadership of laity? Congregations often install leaders to their boards, but they could also confirm leaders of ministry teams through some formal ritual action. This provides a public witness to the call of God and would be a means to invite prayers from the community.

God calls and equips leaders for obedience. It is the responsibility of the Christian leader to cultivate the relationship God establishes through the call. The leader is never alone in this task, but is promised the power and presence of the Holy Spirit. Through the daily disciplines of the faith the Christian leader is equipped to grow in faith and in service.

These first three concentric circles, God, Word, Wisdom, and Call, represent the heart of what it means to be a Christian leader. In the next chapter you will read about the next two concentric circles which, though still included in the "being" component, begin the process of becoming a leader.

Chapter Three: Questions for Reflection

1. How is your relationship with Jesus Christ related to your leadership in the Christian church?
2. What is your congregation's view of Holy Scripture? Is there a document or doctrinal statement; and are your leaders familiar with the statement? Read and reflect on 2 Timothy 3:16-17
3. What does it mean to you that God's Word has power?
4. Can you articulate God's call in your life? The call of the Apostle Paul is recorded in Acts 9. Read and reflect on this passage.
5. How would you explain the transcendence of God?
6. In your opinion, how is God's transcendence an important part of Christian leadership?

Chapter Four

How Do Christian Leaders Grow? "Becoming"

The fourth concentric circle of the Fifth Frame is discipleship and discernment. Specifically, it is at this stage that lay and pastoral leaders pray for discernment of leadership gifts and characteristics. It is also imperative that leaders read scripture, pray, give, study, and develop spiritual relationships.

Discipleship is an exclusive attachment to Jesus Christ. It is obedience to the calling of Jesus Christ and not mere acknowledgement of a doctrinal system. As Bonhoeffer so powerfully stated, "Christianity without the living Christ is inevitably Christianity without discipleship, and Christianity without discipleship is always Christianity without Christ."[97] Obedience requires disciplines of faith. Again, Bonhoeffer wrote:

> Cheap grace is the preaching of forgiveness without requiring repentance, baptism without church discipline, Communion without confession, absolution without personal confession. Cheap grace is grace without discipleship, grace without the cross, grace without Jesus Christ, living and incarnate.[98]

The Christian leader is a disciple first and foremost. Repentance and proper use of God's means of grace strengthen the leader's relationship with Jesus Christ.

Richard Foster outlines twelve distinct spiritual disciplines that "allow us to place ourselves before God so that He can transform us."[99] The disciplines he defines are meditation, prayer, fasting, study, simplicity, solitude, submission, service, confession, worship, guidance, and celebration. Dr. Wayne Goodwin, professor at Gordon-Conwell Seminary Charlotte asked incoming freshmen of the Doctor of Ministry class this question, "When do you worship?" Surprisingly, most answered that question by pointing to times other than when they lead worship in their own congregations. Is it not possible that the leader of worship is also engaged in worship? Devoid of regular worship, a leader is stripped of effectiveness. A parishioner once asked me, "Do you read the Bible every day?" My answer was, "Yes I do," but there was a hesitance as I realized that much of my Bible reading is to prepare for the next sermon, Bible study, or devotional. Clergy and lay leaders alike must practice prayer, scripture reading, and all the other disciplines of faith. Michael Foss calls these "the Marks of Discipleship" and advocates that congregations focus on these in order to grow not only leaders but also the entire body of Christ.[100]

Transformed by God's power, the leader is equipped for leadership. All congregational circumstances can be opportunities for growth in leadership. God uses a variety of means to form the leader including but not limited to, the structures of the church and the processes of mentoring, continuing education, the disciplines of the faith, and even failure.

James Boice highlights three lessons God teaches through failures. No matter how talented the Christian leader, without Jesus Christ he can do nothing. Jesus says, "Apart from me you can do nothing."[101] When a leader fails, God corrects attitudes and reminds him of his dependence on God. It is not the leader's own abilities but the Spirit of God working in the leader. The second lesson is that leaders make major mistakes when they persist in their own way as opposed to the way and will of God. In the book of Acts the Holy Spirit warns Paul not to go to Jerusalem.[102] Then Jesus warns Paul in a vision to get out of Jerusalem. [103] Eventually Paul is arrested and sent to Rome. The third lesson learned from failures is that God can work for the leader and even sometimes in spite of the leader.[104]

The disciple of Jesus Christ seeks the guidance of the Holy Spirit for discernment. Through discernment the Christian leader discovers the gifts given for the building and strengthening of the Christian community. There are a number of spiritual gift inventories that assist laity and clergy in discerning their God given gifts. Too often congregations use the raised hand system of recruitment. The pastor asks for volunteers and the first hand that goes up gets the job. While this may seem like an easy way to recruit potential leaders, it rarely works best.

What are the primary character traits of biblical leaders? A review of the literature reveals a number of leadership characteristics. What follows is a review of the work of a variety of authors and their respective lists.

Phillip Lewis elaborates on ten basic processes and principles that characterize leadership behavior. [105] Citing scriptural references, Lewis highlights such characteristics as persuasion, patience, gentleness, compassionate confrontation, as well as many others.

C. Gene Wilkes illustrates the value of equal relationships among people and warns Christian leaders about what he calls "head-table mentality." He writes, "I had accepted the myth that those who sit at the head table are somehow more important than those who serve in the kitchen."[106] Humility is the first principle of leadership identified by Wilkes. Wilkes identifies seven principles to lead as Jesus led. The principles are, humble your heart, first be a follower, find greatness in service, take risks, take up the towel, share responsibility and authority, and build a team.[107]

Humility is an essential element to Christian leadership. The humble leader understands God is the center of all Christian leadership. Christian leaders who exercise authority with humility prevent arrogance and boasting. Humble authority does not request special privileges. Recall the request of James and John to Jesus. "James and John, the sons of Zebedee, came up to Jesus and asked, "Teacher, will you do us a favor?" Jesus asked them what they wanted, and they answered, "When you come into your glory, please let one of us sit at your right side and the other at your left."[108] Reinhold Niebuhr wrote, "But it would be well if the church realized how dangerous power and prestige are, and how easily they corrupt a man's spiritual integrity."[109]

Using grounded theory research, Rod Jensen uncovered three leadership traits of Martin Luther. They were humility, wisdom, and patience. Humility, however, was central to Luther's leadership model. "Humility for Luther was much more than just a theological abstract or a simple Scriptural admonition on behavior; it was a foundational element of an individual's personality."[110] "Humility to Luther was one of the most esteemed of the divine gifts that could be bestowed upon an individual leader."[111]

Lorin Woolfe set forth ten behaviors and characteristics of biblical leaders. They were honesty and integrity, purpose, kindness and compassion, humility, communication, performance management, team development, courage, justice and fairness, and leadership development.[112] Comparing lists yields common elements in many. Central to all leadership virtues was humility.

In concluding a discourse on the four models of ministry John Stott says that humility is the common denominator in all models. He states that we need humility before Christ, before scripture, before the world and before the congregation.[113] Stott's model for leadership is built around the concept of God's power made perfect in weakness. The Fifth Frame model of leadership places humility as the primary value, the fifth concentric circle.

Even secular leaders recognize the importance of humility as a primary value. Warren Bennis states that the basic virtues of leadership are integrity, dedication, magnanimity, humility, openness, and creativity. He describes humble people in this way:

> They know who they are, have healthy egos, and take more pride in what they do than in who they are. They take accomplishments with a grain of salt and take intelligent criticism without rancor. Such people learn from their mistakes and don't harp on the mistakes of others.[114]

Those who aspire to lead in the church should take note of these words. Accepting intelligent criticism without rancor grows leaders. Leaders in the church who do not harp on the mistakes of others will go a long way in building community.

Two biblical models of leadership, Moses and Jesus, display humility. Scripture states, "Now the man Moses was very humble, more than any man who was on the face of the earth."[115] Paul wrote, "Christ was humble. He obeyed God and even died on a cross. Then God gave Christ the highest place and honored his name above all others."[116] Humility is the fundamental biblical characteristic of leadership. Paul wrote, "For by the grace given to me I bid every one among you not to think of himself more highly than he ought to think, but to think with sober judgment, each according to the measure of faith which God has assigned him."[117] Humility means that the leader does not have too high a view or too low a view of himself or herself. Humility means that the leader has a right understanding of who he or she is in relationship to God and others.

While there are many characteristics of leadership mentioned in scripture and as discussed by Woolfe and Lewis, four are primary. I chose these because they represent well the broad spectrum of leadership and correspond closely with the political, symbolic, human resource, and structural frames.

These four characteristics are diagrammed in a box to illustrate the movement from "being, the core of leadership" to "becoming," the growth of leadership. The concentric circles represent the core of leadership and the boxes represent the behavioral characteristics that are most easily developed with the practice of ministry. It is essential to note that these four primary characteristics of the Fifth Frame model proceed from humility.

The first characteristic is persuasion. Persuasion is the ability to influence someone to do something. Paul wrote that his task is to persuade men.[118] Paul's presentations in the synagogue persuaded many to believe in Jesus.[119] Biblical persuasion is through the power of God. The Apostle Paul wrote:

> When I came to you, brethren, I did not come proclaiming to you the testimony of God in lofty words or wisdom. For I decided to know nothing among you except Jesus Christ and him crucified. And I was with you in weakness and in much fear and trembling; and my speech and my message were not in plausible words of wisdom, but in demonstration of the Spirit and of power, that your faith might not rest in the wisdom of men but in the power of God.[120]

The primary purpose of biblical persuasion is to proclaim the gospel of Jesus Christ. All that the Christian leader does in the management of the congregation must promote the gospel. This is the purpose of the church. Richard Niebuhr wrote that the purpose of the church was to enable people to love one another. The gospel message of salvation in Christ alone compels us to love. Thus while the purpose of the church is the proclamation of the gospel, the Christian leader needs to have a clear vision of what preaching the gospel means in its entirety. Does the church preach the Word and then roll up the pews and go to sleep or is there an expected response?

Dwight Moody, the great evangelist at the turn of the 20th century, preached in the slums of Chicago. In his first attempts to preach to the poor, he took a loaf of bread in one hand and the bible in the other. Moody reported that he dispensed with taking bread because it became a distraction.[121] Does the purpose of the church and its preaching imply physical feeding? Is there a balance?

During Dwight Moody's lifetime another organization, the Salvation Army, emerged. The founders believed that one could not hear the gospel if the stomach was empty. One is reminded of the reported words of St. Francis of Assisi, "Preach the gospel everywhere and, when necessary, use words."

In October of 2005 I had the privilege to work with the Lutheran Disaster Response team for hurricane Katrina victims. The team was headquartered at Christus Victor Lutheran Church, Ocean Springs, Mississippi. My first impression upon walking into the front door of the church was that this is not a church. Inside the narthex were brochures from F.E.M.A. The cry room, a place reserved for parents with infant children, had been converted into a medical triage. In the corner of the narthex was a place to get tetanus shots. Meals were served three times a day in the fellowship hall. The Sunday school area was a shelter where Red Cross workers, volunteers and evacuees were sleeping.

Unable to resist, I asked one of the members, "It looks like the church has been taken over. How are you being the Church?" He replied, "There are some who are troubled by the chaos, but most of us believe we are being the church." The conversation continued but the profound point was made. Is the church not at its best when we preach God's Word and the Word persuades us to service?

The corresponding frame identified by Bolman and Deal which is most akin to the characteristic of persuasion is the symbolic frame. Bolman and Deal assert that the symbolic leader inspires others. It is this trait which is closest to the leadership art of persuasion.

The second characteristic is shrewdness. To be shrewd is to be astute, or sharp; it is someone who is clever and perceptive.[122] The Greek word *phronimos* is often translated as wise. In certain contexts, however, the word connotes shrewd thought. Geoffrey Bromiley writes, "Cunning in the sense of cleverly resolute action in a hopeless situation is the point in Luke 16:8."[123] In this parable Jesus was commending the believer to be clever and to be aware of the dealings of the "sons of this world."[124] Jesus charged his disciples with these words, "Behold, I send you out as sheep in the midst of wolves; therefore be shrewd as serpents, and innocent as doves."[125] The political frame behaviors proceed from the biblical character trait of shrewdness.

This characteristic elicits the most fear among clergy and laity alike. To be shrewd does not mean manipulative. It does not mean building political alliances behind the backs of others. The shrewd leader is aware that there are persons in organizations who do these things. The shrewd leader recognizes behaviors that are deceptive and unproductive. Manipulation is at the top of the list.

One church leader was approached by a member with suggestions for changing the Christmas decorations. The conversation included several options. When the member reported to the Christmas decorations committee, the committee was told that the church leader insisted the change be made. The key word is "insisted." The church leader made several suggestions only to find later that his words were twisted and presented in a dictatorial way. Leaders do not succumb to underhanded tactics nor do they operate as slippery snakes. Leaders deal in fact, truth, and forthrightness. They are to be as innocent as doves, but not so naïve as to not recognize political realities.

Shrewdness is not a trait to fear, but rather a trait to utilize effectively and honestly. The scholar John Killinger understands the need for clergy to be aware of political realities. He writes, "Every church, of whatever size and spiritual persuasion, is a political arena, whether the minister recognizes this or not."[126]

The third characteristic of biblical integrated leadership is understanding. Solomon prays, "Give thy servant therefore an understanding mind to govern thy people, that I may discern between good and evil; for who is able to govern this thy great people?"[127] We should understand as does Solomon that understanding and wisdom comes from God. Consider the words of Proverbs, "For the Lord gives wisdom; from his mouth come knowledge and understanding;"[128] The understanding leader has an ability to see the entire structure of the organization. Another word that fits equally well is "insightful." A leader that is insightful thinks clearly and logically. The leader's thought processes cannot be clouded by human emotions that may unduly influence decisions. The behaviors of the structural frame require a discerning and understanding mind. Understanding comes from hours of prayer and years of experience and ultimately is of God.

The great sculptor Rodin created a statue known as *The Thinker,* to represent thinking as action. He wrote, "What makes my thinker think is that he thinks not only with his brain, with his knitted brow, his distended nostrils and compressed lips, but with every muscle of his arms, back, and legs, with his clenched fists and gripping toes." [129] To be reasonable is to engage the whole person in thinking; it is thinking in action. It is using all of our gifts of insight, all our knowledge, all our intuition, all that God has given us.

The fourth characteristic is compassion. Compassion can be the most misunderstood characteristic. It is not a patronizing pat on the back but a genuine and sincere desire to feel the pain and hurt of another. The word compassion from its origins means "to suffer with."

I had the privilege of working with a team of Christians in the Kairos ministry, a prison ministry in which prison inmates are given a short course in Christianity. The particular prison in which I worked was a high level maximum security penitentiary. The closing ceremony is a time when the microphone is open for any comment. During the closing, one of the residents walked to the podium and said as he fought back tears, "When I came here, I was lonely, lost, and unloved. Now, I have a bunch of friends who love me." He had been showered by the compassion of a group of caring Christian men.

In response to the question, "What shall I do to inherit eternal life?"[130] Jesus told the parable of the Good Samaritan. The mercy that God bestows on his people stirs our hearts for compassion and leads us to respond to people in need.

The behaviors of the human resource frame proceed from the biblical characteristic of compassion.

All four biblical characteristics, persuasion, shrewdness, understanding, and compassion are gifts of God. God works through the power of the Holy Spirit to build up the leader with characteristics needed for leading. Leaders are guided by the power of the Holy Spirit. God's Spirit strengthens the church for effective witness and unity. Luther wrote,

> But the Holy Spirit has called me through the Gospel, enlightened me with his gifts, and sanctified and preserved me in true faith, just as he calls, gathers, enlightens, and sanctifies the whole Christian church on earth and preserves it in union with Jesus Christ in the one true faith. [131]

The Holy Spirit can and will speak to us and enlighten us with gifts. One summer I offered a class on prayer in which we studied fundamentals such as adoration, confession, intercession, and finally meditation. On the last day, after a time of scripture reading, the group spent approximately twenty minutes in silent meditation listening for an insight from God. As I pondered the group, the scripture, and the fellowship we enjoyed during the week, God renewed my confidence in his ability to create community. I heard a clear confirmation that it is God who unites people in faith. Too often I felt as though I had to build the relationships, encourage the fellowship, and create community.

All too often clergy and lay leaders work as if they are the only ones stirring the hearts of God's people. The Holy Spirit will help you discern your gifts for leadership and equip you with Fifth Frame characteristics. For instance consider that some individuals are very persuasive. Those who gravitate toward sales positions can utilize their persuasive ability in the work of God's church. I remember some years ago when a parishioner said to me that I had, in his words, "done a sale job on the congregation." The comment was delivered in scorn as if it is a bad thing to persuade someone to act.

Other individuals are naturally gifted at working for consensus and compromise. Shrewd individuals need not be derided but rather encouraged to assist in keeping communications open and straightforward. Extremely compassionate individuals work well with outreach and ministries to the hurting and homeless, but are less effective at long range planning. Each person works with unique characteristics and utilizes unique God –given leadership behaviors. The key, however, is teamwork.

What characteristics does your leadership team possess? Is your board of elders, deacons, or council, aware of the need to have a balanced leadership team? Identify your traits and those of your team and get into the world and lead people into a vibrant and active relationship with a living and powerful God.

Chapter Four: Questions for Reflection

1. What does discipleship mean to you? What does it mean to your church? Read and reflect on John 6: 65-69.

2. Do the leaders of your congregation encourage members to worship, pray, read scripture, and give of their resources?

3. How has your congregation failed and what lessons were learned?

4. What method does your congregation use to match volunteers to ministries? Read 1 Corinthians 12: 27-30.

5. Review the various lists of character traits of biblical leaders. What list would you make of your traits? Your congregations?

6. What does it mean to be humble? Read and reflect on Philippians 2: 1-11.

7. When have you or your congregational leaders used the leadership of persuasion? Shrewdness? Understanding? Compassion?

Chapter Five

How do Christians Lead?
"Doing"

While history is brimming with leaders, the Old Testament is filled with men and women who did extraordinary work in God's service. Of all of the leaders of scripture and even of those who have left legacies in secular history, no two are more archetypical than Moses and Jesus. While these two primary leaders in Holy Scripture are discussed at length in numerous texts, the unique slant of this chapter is to reveal their leadership characteristics in light of Bolman and Deal's concept of four frames. How do these two men exercise leadership, and how does it demonstrate the symbolic, structural, human resource, and political categories of leadership?

Specifically, did these two leaders identify, organize, plan, and allocate the resources of time, money, materials, facilities, and human resources? This question is similar to the perspective of the political frame. Second, how were their interpersonal skills, especially regarding team member participation, teaching and coaching, servant leadership, and ethnic diversity? This is the essence of the human resource frame. Third, what was their ability to acquire, evaluate, organize, maintain, interpret, and communicate information? The most important task for the symbolic leader is to inspire through stories, slogans, and symbols. Fourth, did they understand and design complex interrelationships (or organizational systems)?[132] Structural leaders understand the systems necessary to accomplish the task. How do the leadership of Moses and Jesus address these questions?

Rabbi David Baron identifies fifty leadership lessons from the Moses narrative, and suggests that the leadership of Moses also refutes the five well-known management myths.[133] In some sense there is a mystique that surrounds all discussions of leadership. It is as if there is a great aura that envelopes all great leaders and they possess some magic.

Leaders possess no magic formula, but defined characteristics and a specific skill set. For instance the first management myth is that leadership is a rare skill. The assumption underlying this falsehood is that there are very few people who really lead and that leadership is an inherent skill. Christian leaders know that God is our source and thus there is no limit to who God will call to lead. The second myth is that leaders are born and not made. This defies all logic for the Christian leader. I recall the words of John the Baptist when he said to the Pharisees and Sadducees, "God is able from these stones to raise up children to Abraham." God can and does make and form leaders. The third management sham is that leaders are charismatic. History is marked by great leaders in business, industry, and churches that are upon first appearance dull. Another deception that persists is that leadership exists only at the top of an organization. Finally there is the myth that leaders control, direct, prod, and manipulate.[134]

What are the leadership characteristics of Moses? Moses exhibits inspirational leadership when communicating the Ten Commandments. Baron writes, "Reading the commands aloud, writing them down, establishing a special place for them, reciting them again – this is how Moses reinforced his message and infused the Israelites with the ideals of Judaism."[135] This ritualistic action is a great way to communicate and is a style most often used by symbolic leaders. For example, Moses made two silver trumpets to gather the people and for breaking camp.[136]

The items inside the tent of meeting were symbols that communicated on a spiritual level. The bronze basin, for example, contained water for washing and was placed between the tent of meeting and the altar. Hands and feet were to be washed when Aaron and his sons came near the altar and when they made an offering. Just how important is it to wash your hands and feet? One might think this is an important ritual but certainly not one with deadly consequences. Yet, the scripture states, "They shall wash their hands and feet, so that they may not die: it shall be a perpetual ordinance for them."[137]

The most visual symbol of the people, of course, was the Ark of the Covenant. As the Ark went before the people Moses would say, "Arise, O Lord, let your enemies be scattered, and your foes flee before you." When the Ark came to rest, Moses would say, "Return, O Lord of the ten thousand thousands of Israel."[138] The Ark was a powerful reminder of God's presence and power. On one occasion the power of the Ark was unleashed on Uzzah who touched the ark and died.

Structurally, Moses put in place a chain of command so he would not get bogged down in the minutia of daily details. Can you imagine the daily dose of disputes, quarrels, and accidents he encountered leading thousands of people? There was no 911 operator standing nearby in the event of an emergency. Remember, these people were wandering in the wilderness, a place of danger, and each day was filled with more challenge than we moderns can possibly imagine.

Into this mixture of mayhem and madness comes Jethro, Moses' father-in-law, who has heard how Moses has brought the people out of Egypt. Jethro witnesses the daily grind and daily judging duties of Moses. Jethro asks Moses why he is spending all of his time doing this. God called Moses to lead the people to the Promised Land and not to be the sole arbiter in the Land of Petty disputes.

Jethro reminds him that if he continues to lead in this manner he will wear himself out. He offers sage advice, along with the words, "and may God be with you..." an obvious clue that God is working through Jethro.

Jethro replied: That isn't the best way to do it. [18] You and the people who come to you will soon be worn out. The job is too much for one person; you can't do it alone. [19] God will help you if you follow my advice. You should be the one to speak to God for the people, [20] and you should teach them God's laws and show them what they must do to live right. [21] You will need to appoint some competent leaders who respect God and are trustworthy and honest. Then put them over groups of ten, fifty, a hundred, and a thousand. [22] These judges can handle the ordinary cases and bring the more difficult ones to you. Having them to share the load will make your work easier. [23] This is the way God wants it done. You won't be under nearly as much stress, and everyone else will return home feeling satisfied.[139]

This incident demonstrates some important principles. Sometimes leaders can get so bogged down in the details that they fail to work toward the big picture, the vision and mission of the organization. It also shows that leaders need to listen to the advice given by trusted wise advisors, even when they do not want to hear it and think they are doing the right thing. Listening closely to and heeding the counsel of others is an act of humility. Indeed, in this instance, Jethro's advice made complete sense. Consider the circumstances, what was more important: to get to the Promised Land or to listen to lawsuits all day in the desert? It was time to delegate authority through a structural framework to handle the petty disputes so that the nation of Israel could get on with God's business.

Moses deals cleverly with conflict and opposition. It probably comes as a surprise to many that Moses would have defiance in the ranks. Who could dare to disobey this noble man of faith? Of course, some may recall the incident with the golden calf. Moses ascended the mountain to talk with God and as he descended he beheld the people worshipping a golden calf.

Stopping in his tracks, Moses broke the tablets. This episode, however, was just the beginning of the people's disobedience.

In another instance, 250 leaders rose up against Moses. The scripture reports, "And they rose up before Moses, with a number of the people of Israel, two hundred and fifty leaders of the congregation, chosen from the assembly, well-known men..." [140] What would any lay or clergy leader do in the face of such strong opposition? I recall a newspaper article in which a college president prayed for God to "smite his enemies." Somehow it does not seem reasonable to expect God to smite our enemies or to open the earth and swallow contentious church members.

In this situation, the first thing Moses did was knelt down and prayed. Then, Moses told Korah and his company to wait until morning. The next morning the Lord opened the ground and Korah and his company was swallowed up with everything they owned. There are specific steps that are discernable and practical for any leader facing such a monumental challenge. Moses prayed, waited, and faced the conflict with God by his side.

One clergy leader told me once that his objective in all potentially conflicting matters is to demonstrate a calming presence. What would happen, however, if instead of a calming presence, pastors and other lay leaders immediately hoped for the earth to swallow the problem? Imagine the scene, the earth swallowing the antagonist. This might seem comforting to some and a quick way to address problems, but it is not the most desirable outcome. The leadership in this situation is best described as political savvy. Rabbi Baron writes:

> His first move was to stall for time by telling everyone to return the next morning and see how the conflict would be resolved. However, he didn't postpone resolution for long, only until the next day. [141]

Another pastor reported that divisive conflict in his congregation began over altar flowers a year before he began his ministry there. Sides were chosen in the manner of the Hatfields and McCoys and the conflict permeated the entire congregation. Deciding to address the matriarch of the congregation who was embittered and involved in the entire scenario, the pastor went to her home. He reported that she unloaded all of her anger on him and by the time he left her home, she had accused him of being responsible for all of the conflict. The car ride home was long and painful as he reflected on the conflict and felt it was his fault. Determined to quit the ordained ministry, he heard the still small voice speaking to his heart: "God called you!" The strength for conflict comes from God and God's call to the leader. This strength is akin to the staff in the shepherd's hand; it can strike fear in the heart of those who would arbitrarily challenge authority.

Strength in the face of trials, however, is never easy. On March 27th of 2005, a Presbyterian minister friend and I, along with five men and seven high school boys began a trek of 25 miles on the Appalachian Trail. The excitement built rapidly as we arrived at our appointed camp site for the first evening. Reality, however, sank in as we faced howling winds and blowing rain the first night. The next morning as winds and rain stopped, we left our cars and put our boots to the trail with the expectation of reaching the pinnacle of our hike, Albert Mountain.

Nothing could have prepared me for what happened on the first full day of hiking. Sleet turned to snow as bitterly cold winds moved in. It was Monday afternoon and one young man became ill. He and one of our leaders turned back. By Monday evening the cold had taken its toll. I felt like Captain Bligh surrounded by a mutinous crew. Even the adults were challenging the itinerary. "Let's go back" became the mantra of almost everyone.

The Reverend Dr. Ken Thomas and I had put this trip together and we did not want to turn back. We listened to the groaning and the reasons why we should turn back. After evening devotions, we settled in with the agreement to wait until morning to decide. My prayer was for a clear morning and warmer weather. When the Tuesday morning sun poked over the mountains, the air was warm and the sunshine was bright. It was a new day, the potential mutiny passed, and we decided to march onward to our destination, Albert Mountain. When we eventually got to the top of the mountain the view was as breathtaking as I had remembered on a previous hike, but the thrill was even deeper. I rejoiced as everyone, especially the teenagers, celebrated their physical and mental achievement.

"Let's go back" is often the slogan of church members who long for the supposed security of a more comfortable time. When the leader has seen the view from the mountain and experienced the excitement, the leader can only work through the potential discord and continue to lead the people forward because he knows that the achievement is worthy of the challenge. As Moses stood on the mountain overlooking the Promised Land, he no doubt knew that his leadership efforts were justified.

Leading the people through the wilderness in anticipation of the Promised Land was not easy for Moses. The Israelites, just like those young men in our hike, had not seen the destination. Moses led with strength but also had to listen carefully, care for gently, and support prayerfully the wandering Israelites.

He demonstrated the depth of his care when he came down from Mount Sinai. There Moses had spoken with God and received the Ten Commandments. These laws brought order to the people and later influenced the laws of many nations. Moses, however, went from the mountaintop to the valley of despair, for down below people were worshipping a golden calf. While he was talking to the one God, the people made a golden god. God's response to their disobedience was swift and decisive. God's desire was to destroy the people and make a great nation with Moses. Again, Moses prays for the people.

> The next day Moses told the people, 'This is a terrible thing you have done. But I will go back to the LORD to see if I can do something to keep this sin from being held against you.' Moses returned to the LORD

and said, 'The people have committed a terrible sin. They have made a gold idol to be their god. But I beg you to forgive them. If you don't, please wipe my name out of your book. [142]

Initially, Moses was angry with the people, angry enough to discard the two stone tablets and break them into pieces. Surprisingly, Moses' anger did not last, but instead Moses pleaded for his people. Considering all the complaining that the people of Israel had done and the challenges they had placed before Moses, why did he not just take God up on his offer to wipe them out? Baron writes of this incident, "It's a tempting offer: Get rid of the whining and uncooperative Israelites and let God create a whole new nation out of Moses' own progeny." [143]

Inspiration, public rituals, shared authority, a clear structure, wisdom in conflict, and deep concern and support for the people are fundamental components of leadership. These traits, seen clearly in the leadership of Moses, are examples of the integrated leadership of Bolman and Deal. Moses demonstrated structural leadership in his ability to share authority and establish a company of judges. Moses exhibited political leadership traits in his ability to face conflict. Moses used symbolic leadership in his use of rituals. As a human resource leader, Moses prayed for his people even when God wanted to abandon them.

What leadership traits did Jesus demonstrate in the face of conflict and opposition? The second and third chapters of Mark relate what one scholar calls the five conflict stories, so called because Jesus stood squarely against the religious rulers of his day.

D.E. Nineham proposed two ideas that single out these texts as "conflict stories." He writes; "They show that opposition to Jesus came not from the ordinary Jewish people, but from authorities who had religious vested interests to maintain; and they make clear the true character and grounds of the opposition, showing that it arose entirely from misunderstanding and shortcoming on the part of the authorities, and not at all from any fault on the part of Jesus."[144]

Take for instance the fifth so-called "conflict" story in which Jesus enters the synagogue to heal a man with a withered hand. The religious rulers carefully watched Jesus to see if he would heal on the Sabbath, and when he did, Jesus confronted them with a question: "Is it lawful to do good or to do harm on the Sabbath, to save life or to kill?"[145] In response, they were silent.

This conflict story demonstrates Jesus ability to face conflict constructively. Jesus knows the intentions of the Pharisees and the eventual conflict. Jesus knows the Pharisees are an opposing major constituency. The political reality is that the Pharisees are not getting what they want from Jesus. All political scenarios recognize the presence of limited resources. The limited resource in this case is the power of the Pharisees administered through an exclusive religious system. This was their "vested interest" as Nineham identified the conflict. Jesus confronts the inadequacies of this system by healing on the Sabbath.

Later in the gospel of Mark Jesus encountered a different sort of opposition in a man possessed by an evil spirit[146] and demonstrated persuasive leadership. Nineham writes, "The primary point of this story... was to stress the overwhelming power available to Jesus in his contest with the demonic powers."[147] Mark writes, "For he had often been bound with fetters and chains, but the chains he wrenched apart, and the fetters he broke in pieces; *and no one had the strength to subdue him*."[148] (Italics added) The man with an evil spirit was representative of the force of evil. The stage was set for Jesus to confront the evil, the force in direct opposition to Jesus' work. In the text, Jesus defeated the evil and enlisted the man for work in the Kingdom of God. Jesus instructed the man by saying, "Go home to your friends, and tell them how much the Lord has done for you, and how he has had mercy on you." [149] The man went into the Decapolis to tell what Jesus had done for him.

Jesus entry into Jerusalem on a donkey symbolized his humility and servant hood. In the gospel of John, Jesus washed the disciples' feet as a symbol of his servant hood. The focal point of Jesus service is summed up in Matthew 20:28 "just as the Son of Man came not to be served but to serve, and to give his life a ransom for many." The entry into Jerusalem served as the definitive symbolic event for Jesus ministry of service that culminated in his crucifixion in Jerusalem.

The Last Supper was an event that Jesus transformed into a new meal with new meaning. What was once a meal to commemorate the Exodus from Egypt and formerly known as Passover, Jesus refashioned into a meal to commemorate his exodus from earth and our freedom from sin. Jesus used the symbols of bread and wine, familiar to his followers, and gave them new meaning. Jesus, through this meal, forms a unique identity for the church separate and distinct from the Jewish religion. The Last Supper was a ritual in the best sense of the term.

Bolman and Deal suggest rituals are important to organizations and serve four roles: to socialize, to stabilize, to reduce anxieties and ambiguities, and to convey messages to external constituencies.[150] The Eucharistic meal of bread and wine demonstrates all four. The meal socializes by bringing people together around a sacred meal with Jesus as host. It provides stability by linking the Christian church to the past event known as the Passover. For the believer, the meal provides a peace that strengthens resolve and assists in the battle with earthly anxieties. Finally, the meal conveys a message of unity and invitation to all unbelievers since all Christians celebrate the meal.

The story of Jesus walking on water shows Jesus' power. While the apocalyptic writings in Daniel and Revelation depict great beasts rising up out of the sea, Jesus' miraculous power to walk on water symbolically demonstrates power over the demons of the deep and his mission to thwart the forces of evil.

Jesus demonstrated his leadership when he performed miracles which revealed his deep concern for his people. Jesus performed miracles to build faith and to draw individuals into the life giving Word. One day while a great crowd was following Jesus, a leader of the synagogue named Jairus fell at his feet and begged repeatedly, "My daughter is at the point of death. Come and lay your hands on her, so that she may be made well and live."[151] Jairus, by the nature of his office, was accustomed to people asking him for favors and yet he fell on his knees and asked Jesus for a miracle. Clearly, an authority emanated from Jesus.

When Jesus fed the five thousand, he did more than provide for the mere physical needs of the people. Since eating together was considered an intimate affair, Jesus brought the crowd together in fellowship through this miracle to build community and strengthen relationships.

Jesus led by equipping and empowering others for service in his ministry. For example, Jesus sent out the disciples two by two. This served to underscore Jesus' mission as a mission of the church rather than an individual mission. Eduard Schweizer writes, "Service for Jesus is always service in the church and can never be done by only one person. The teamwork of at least two is a symbol of this truth."[152] This is the organizational model for the work of the church, the structure that Jesus set at the beginning of mission work. The structure was clear. There was no confusion about the goals of the mission. The disciples were to preach that persons should repent.

This clear structure and well-defined goals are the hallmark of what Bolman and Deal categorize as structural leadership. Other traits such as dealing with conflict constructively, the use of symbolism, inspiration and persuasion, the performance of miracles, demonstrate that the four frame behaviors of integrated leadership are used by Jesus, as well as Moses.

What about clergy and lay leaders and four frame leadership? How do Christian leaders use the Word of God as a model for their own leadership and incorporate the four frames of Bolman and Deal? As you reflect on your own situation and the leaders in your congregation, what examples come to mind? Consider the following pastors and their demonstration of leadership in a variety of ministry settings. Let us begin with the symbolic leader.

The task of the symbolic leader is to inspire people and give them something in which to believe. The Christian symbolic leader understands that inspiration comes from the Holy Spirit and cannot be controlled or contrived. This leader points to the symbols of the faith, inspires through the story of Christ, and leads by creating a culture of humility and obedience.

A biblical classic of inspiring leadership is recorded in the 17th chapter of Exodus. Moses sends an army to battle Amalek while he stands on the top of a hill holding the staff of God. As Moses' hands lower, Amalek prevails in battle; so Aaron and Hur hold up his hands. Did the Israelites defeat Amalek and his people in part due to the inspiration of Moses? It was not the prowess and perceived strength that inspired the troops below, but rather an innate trust that Moses, a humble man, was called by God to lead them.

Through the use of a survey, a 76 year old downtown Lutheran congregation discovered that they were perceived as not being good neighbors. The pastor initiated renewal through the use of symbolic leadership. First, he appointed, "The Spirit of 76 Committee." Through the use of many surveys, the congregation developed a pecking order for the priority of needs and the committee used this to develop brochures and slogans.

Massive work was begun on the landscape. The symbol of this project became an old prayer garden altar. The altar was moved from a back corner of the grounds to out in front of the buildings. The old altar was made up from the stones from the first stone sanctuary. The cross was made from the stones outside of the church and the cornerstone.

The altar is now in the front and center of the newly renovated prayer garden. Benches were placed in the garden. Today, it is a place where the children play and people walk by to get to the education wing. The pastor remarked, "Renewal came from the old stuff, but casting it into a new structure and a new place and saying, let's move on." Funds were solicited for this project from one-dollar increments to several thousand-dollar contributions. For example, prices were suggested for shrubbery, trees and other landscaping items in order to increase participation. Symbolically, parishioners could say, " I bought one bush."

The secular human resource leader believes that people are the heart of the organization and that people are loyal and committed when the organization is responsive to their needs. The Christian human resource leader believes that God creates the people of the church and that the true heart of the organization is Jesus. Since the church is the body of Christ, the organization is not so much responsive to their needs as much as they are a part of the body of Christ. The Christian human resource leader teaches loyalty and commitment by "preaching Christ crucified."[153]

This is in stark contrast to the ever present mantra to meet people's needs in order to bring them into the kingdom of God. Certainly, there is a place for meeting needs, but the church gives what people need by asking them to deny themselves. I recall the conversation of an individual who expressed great dissatisfaction with his church by stating, "I am not being spiritually fed in this congregation." Similarly, a parishioner informed her pastor that she found his sermons seriously lacking and so was staying home to watch the "preacher" on television, to which he replied, "Call him the next time you are in the hospital." While this sounds harsh, spiritual needs are met in the rough and tumble of community.

One pastor of a 1400 member congregation, faced with the overwhelming task of getting to know his parishioners, implemented neighborhood gatherings. He set aside Tuesday night to meet at a host home in order to meet people and talk with them about their lives and their aspirations for the congregation. He emphasized a desire to listen to people's stories of faith. This approach solidified beliefs that congregants are members of one body, the body of Christ.

The secular political leader recognizes political reality, manages conflict, develops ties to leadership, and works for compromise. The Christian political leader never limits God or his power to expand ministry. Christian political leaders realize that sometimes there is no need to negotiate for supposedly limited resources. A favorite phrase of one parishioner is, "Let's give God a chance to do a miracle among us." Conflict is managed primarily through prayer and humble obedience. Compromise for the Christian political leader begins with compassionate listening in dialogue with one another and with the understanding that God is always present when two or three gather in his name. The Christian political leader seeks to discern not the will of the people but rather the will of God in all conflict.

As defined here, political leadership does not sound so bad. Most individuals believe that politics have no place in the church. What they mean, in part, is that the strong arm tactics of compromise too often weaken the mission of the church. There is no compromise regarding the gospel and its proclamation.

One pastor in our study worked for many years with the local telephone company where he learned a leadership behavior that he utilized in his parish. He kept one particular congregant well informed because this person was, as he called him, an "opinion former." In his experience in the telephone business, he always spoke to "opinion formers" in select towns prior to major change in the industry, and in effect they helped him shape changes.

In an effort to shape changes many Christian leaders encounter those who embrace change and those who resist. Some draw the distinction between "church people" and "chapel people." Church people are those who want to do outreach and who wish to take seriously the Great Commission. The chapel people are those who want a good experience on Sunday morning and who want the church to take care of them. One might describe this as the maintenance group, while the word "mission" describes the church group.

The political reality is that both groups have to co-exist. Chapel people are generally the ones who have been members for a long time and are the ones who have the bulk of the financial resources. You have to solicit permission from the chapel people since they have the influence and the resources in order for outreach to take place. Perhaps the hesitancy seen in the chapel people is their fear of the power shift that can occur in the organization upon the arrival of new people. This is a genuine political reality for many established congregations and calls for compassionate, yet wise, leadership.

The structural leader clarifies goals and works to build an effective structure responsive to the environment. The Christian structural leader provides goals for the church through the Great Commission and the Great Commandment. The entire structure of the church is centered on images of the church as the body of Christ with Christ as the head.

Structure can impede or enhance the expansion of the Kingdom of God. Some congregations implement outreach through endowment funds. One congregation made significant changes in their endowment fund structure in order to distribute more funds. In this congregation, one person controlled the money for the first fifteen years of the fund which included the buying and selling of all stock. The pastor and congregation set up a group to study and identify the risks and parameters for the foundation. The next task was to seek a committee to manage the investments according to those parameters.

In effect, the outcome was ideal. Those who invested well were part of one group while the other group was composed of individuals who enjoyed giving away money. The group that enjoyed finding ministries with which to share funds made presentations and requests to the foundation. The final step in this entire process was the development of a document of philosophy and procedures that included such specific goals as growing the corpus of the endowment at one or two percent above the determined percentage of the "cost of living." It also set the goal of giving away at least five percent of the foundation's resources each year.

Christian leadership is built on a core belief in God and grows as the leader discerns and develops leadership characteristics. The practice of leadership flows from the core foundation. The fifth frame is provided as a visual model. It is important to note that the lines are drawn connecting all boxes. The entire model is interconnected in many ways because the Holy Spirit works in and within each and every process constantly guiding and directing the leader.

The model encompasses essential components of Christian leadership with the foundation in God. The Word of God reveals God's son Jesus Christ and provides guidance through God's will. God initiates the call to the believer. It is the responsibility of the leader to utilize the disciplines of the faith for growth in discipleship and discernment of gifts. Humility influences all the thoughts and processes of the leader. Proceeding from this core and guided by the Holy Spirit are the four primary characteristics of persuasion, shrewdness, understanding, and compassion. The behaviors of the four frames proceed from these characteristics. While no Christian leader can be extremely proficient with all four characteristics and behavioral frames, Christian leaders can be aware of all aspects of the Fifth Frame and build effective teams to engage leadership from all perspectives.

The entire model encompasses much of what is written in Christian literature regarding leadership. The model includes the components of who we are as leaders at the core of our being, how we grow and become leaders, and finally how we practice and do leadership. The core of the Fifth Frame consists of the five concentric circles and corresponds to the "being" portion of leadership, the core of who leaders are. The second section, the attribute of "becoming," begins with discipleship, one of the central circles, and is seen primarily in the four primary characteristics. Each Christian leader grows in the formation of these character traits. The final section, the behaviors of the four frames, comprises the "doing" component and the practice of leadership.

How will the elders, deacons, vestry or council in your congregation develop effective structures, recognize the political realities, implement human resource tools, and utilize the symbols of the faith in a way that rally the congregation? The task before the reader is to identify the leaders and their skills and put them in ministries best served by their God given talents. A team of leaders who understand all the dynamics of the Fifth Frame and who lead with humility can impact the kingdom of God in a powerful way. Are you ready to build a powerful team of leaders?

Chapter Five: Questions for Reflection

1. What passages of scripture demonstrates the symbolic leadership of Moses? What about political, structural, and human resource?

2. What is your congregation's "chain of command?" Does it work well?

3. Read once more Exodus 18: 17-23. How might the leaders of your congregation establish a structure that lessens the load for everyone?

4. How have you and the leaders in your congregation handled opposition?

5. Can you maintain a "calming presence" when your leadership is challenged?

6. Discuss the leadership of Jesus. How is he a political leader? Symbolic? Structural? Human Resource?

7. What examples of leadership successes have you enjoyed? Your congregation?

Chapter Six

Visionary Leadership and the Fifth Frame

There was a time when any discussion of leadership automatically included visioning. I remember a news conference in which a newly selected C.E.O. of International Business Machines was asked about a new vision and he replied that the last thing IBM needed was a vision. His words shocked the legions of vision gurus. Christian leaders believe that vision is essential for the leadership of a congregation and often cite Proverbs 29: 18, "Where there is no vision the people perish."

While no one expects the church to perish, we need to ask: What is the identity of the Christian church in the United States? Do the unchurched know that churches are a place for spiritual growth and houses of prayer? While there is a wide diversity of worship practice and theological doctrines, Christ is present and he desires salvation and wholeness for his people. Yet, no church is immune to the struggles affecting Methodists, Lutherans, Presbyterians, and Episcopalians as well as other denominations.

What is the purpose of the Church? This question is most important for mainline congregations. The Lutheran denomination has suffered decline during the last three decades in membership growth and financial contributions. Some might even say that there is a crisis of morale. What was once a church of great promise and grand opportunity has seemingly become a church in survival mode struggling to find its identity. Richard

Cimino concurs that while the 1950's are viewed by some as the golden age for American Lutheranism, the most recent years have given serious challenge to the identity of Lutheranism in the United States.[154]

One place to begin in shaping identity and creating energy for ministry is by forming a compelling vision. The primary focus of this vision needs to be leadership because the Great Commission (Matthew 28: 9-20) commands the church to make disciples and empower them to lead. The vision must have an easily understandable doctrine of the Word and a biblical model of leadership as its core.

The lack of identity and vision is one reason the book by Rick Warren, *The Purpose Driven Church*, has been so helpful to many Christian churches. It addresses the need for congregations to be clear about their identity as Christian congregations and to identify their purposes. He writes: "Every church needs to grow warmer through fellowship, deeper through discipleship, stronger through worship, broader through ministry, and larger through evangelism."[155] There should be no guesswork on the part of visitors to our churches about what we believe and who we are as people of God.

Newberry College has a creed posted on walls around its campus. It reads:

> *"As a Newberrian I will honor the code of honesty in my academic and social life. I will respect the rights of every other member of this community as a person and creature of God. I will actively support the rights of others as a keystone to ensuring the integrity of Newberry College as a place of free and open inquiry."*[156]

The handbook further states that by affixing one's signature to this statement, the individual will live and work within the Christian environment of Newberry College. When I attended the initial orientation with my daughter, I was thankful for the clear words of the college president. He said that Newberry was a Christian college and espoused Christian values; if persons were uncomfortable with these values, they might want to consider another institution.

Does your congregation have a clear vision of expectations? One person shared with me what her pastor said during a new member class; he said in a loving but straightforward manner that individuals should expect to serve when joining the church and if they were not interested in serving, they should seek another congregation.

Do we have high expectations for God's Word to change us? Does the transforming vision force us to ask, "Are we affecting the world for the Kingdom of God?" Lutherans, as well as many other mainline denominations, have suffered from what some call an increasingly secular agenda. Peter Berger writes, "There has been an all too easy identification of Christian faith with sets of secular values and secular agendas. This was a distortion of the gospel then, as it is a distortion now."[157] Foremost to this secularization is identification with leadership models that work well in industry and business but lack a biblical basis for Christian use. This secularization along with other factors has contributed to a numerical decline as well as in some sense a spiritual decline. Adopting a comprehensive biblical leadership development model should revitalize the church's vision.

The symbolic frame, with the attending biblical characteristic of persuasion, is where vision is created. The research of Lee Bolman and Terrence Deal underscores the needed development of symbolic leadership. They write that high performance and effective teamwork is linked to ritual, play, ceremony, and myth and they highlight keys of symbolic leadership.[158] Most of these have value and meaning for Christian congregations when considered in light of the Fifth Frame. Together these keys can be very helpful in building a compelling vision. Consider seven of these keys in light of the Fifth Frame and how you might use them in building a vision for your congregation.

The first key is "How someone becomes a team member is important." The core values of the Fifth Frame leadership model along with other values specific to a congregation should be communicated up front before someone joins a congregation. Congregations need to invite people to a serious faith. If the congregational model is "come on in and we will teach you later," the leaders communicate that joining the team requires no effort and no commitment. There was a time in Christian history when there was a season of learning and preparation and congregations prayed for those discerning membership. If we are to inculcate faith, we must take a serious look at how individuals join the team. The Fifth Frame model of leadership with its emphasis on discipleship and discernment is the beginning of this process.

"Diversity gives a team a competitive advantage," is the second key. Diversity of ideas for ministry is always welcome such as a team that welcomes diverse viewpoints on how to reach the unchurched. The Fifth Frame of leadership recognizes that there are those who are persuasive, shrewd, understanding and compassionate. All of these characteristics plus patience, gentleness, kindness and so many others are needed to build an effective team. The Apostle Paul wrote, "Indeed, the body does not consist of one member but of many."[159] He wrote these words to the Corinthians reminding them that each part of the body is important. Clearly, God made each person unique so why not build our teams around our God given differences?

The third key is "Example rather than command holds a team together." People follow leaders who are willing to do what they expect others to do. For example, when I was in college I worked for Alexander's Catalog Showroom, a retail store. The manager, Mr. Hurd was a strong leader, but he also set a strong example by assisting other employees in their work. He was never immune to moving merchandise, mopping floors, or whatever else was necessary. People called him Mr. Hurd not because it was a title given, but because he had earned the title.

How might the leaders of congregations lead by example and set a tone of humble service for the entire body of Christ? Can our visions be so clear as to inspire shrewdness, compassion, understanding, and persuasion? We need teams of leaders committed to spreading the gospel and setting a positive example in reaching people with the good news of Jesus Christ. Barked commands do not motivate. I remember well a slogan I once saw in a store window: "A pint of example is worth a pound of advice." A small expression of love multiplied by the power of God can move mountains and is more valued than unsolicited advice.

The fourth key states that a specialized language fosters cohesion and commitment. People are motivated for service when they feel connected. Via de Cristo is a leadership training and spiritual development tool of the Lutheran church. Unique to the movement is its language. For instance those who attend a retreat for the first time are dubbed "pilgrims." Those who serve pilgrims while they are seated at tables are called "chas." "Ultreyas" are celebration events. While these words may seem a hindrance to some, they build cohesiveness.

While conversing with a colleague about ministry he remarked, "You and I were trained to think theologically." For the better part of my first three years of parish ministry, I often thought psychologically. I used terms like rapport, conditioning, shaping, and positive reinforcement. Pastors and church leaders, however, need to use the language of the church. And while the Christian church has a large vocabulary of words mostly unknown to those unaffiliated, these words tie people together as do common values. Leaders need common theological words for discussion and dialogue. The call of God, the Word of God, Discipleship, Discernment of gifts, and humility are the language of the Fifth Frame. These words along with the Christian characteristics of leadership form a common language for leaders.

What if we elected people to our boards and other positions of leadership who were expected to articulate God's call in their life rather than simply electing individuals who have leadership positions in the secular realm? Christian leaders need to be able to articulate their call to service and their feelings of humility before God. Congregational boards need to have discussions about what it means to be a disciple and how our relationship with Jesus Christ is central to our leadership in the Church.

What about our understanding of the Word of God? Don't we believe that it has the power to change lives? As for the characteristics of leadership, are we willing to face the reality of political processes? Dare we be shrewd in our service in the Kingdom of God? Leadership teams need to learn the Christian leadership language and debate among themselves and within their Christian community what these terms mean. Do we not deeply desire disciples who work together with commitment, camaraderie, and a common language of Christian leadership?

The fifth symbolic key states that stories carry history and values. In his book *The Life Cycle of Congregations,* Martin Saarinen writes: "Decline may be arrested by tapping the life sources inherent in the birth story of the congregation."[160] Congregations can renew their energy for mission by recalling their birth story. How did the congregation begin and what circumstances and challenges were present? Dr. Carl Honeycutt, a supply pastor for St. James Lutheran Church over thirty years ago was often quoted as saying, "I know the devil has been in St. James because I have seen his footprints." This story communicates a value, although perhaps not one a congregation wishes to remember. The challenges inherent in not only birthing a congregation, but sustaining it in the face of certain opposition from wicked spiritual forces are tremendous. Congregational histories are filled with stories that enlighten and help us recall our roots.

In my second parish we buried a time capsule in commemoration of the church's 75th anniversary. The ceremony that surrounded the event gave parishioners time to reflect positively on the past and look hopefully to the future. When the time capsule is opened, parishioners can retell the stories of the past and remember that God is faithful. Dr. Robert Hawkins, professor at Lutheran Theological Southern Seminary prepared a liturgy to be used in the burial of a time capsule that states, "Therefore, in this 175th year of the seminary's ministry, we set apart these objects, dear to us and reminders to those who follow, of our work to be faithful stewards of God's gifts in this place."[161] Stories of God's guidance in the life of a congregation need to be told so that others may be edified. Willow Creek church celebrated its 30th anniversary in 2006. Senior Pastor Bill Hybels remarked, "We marked our 30th anniversary by celebrating 30 years of everyday people finding God." The author of the article, Susan DeLay continued, "Everyone has a story and every story has meaning."[162] Stories of faith energize our actions and remind us of God's power.

The sixth key states that humor can reduce tension and encourage creativity. This is central to the fellowship life of a congregation. A number of the congregations in Sumter, South Carolina, prepare videos for the local Crimestoppers Telethon. Many of them evoke sidesplitting laughter not only for viewers, but members as well. Teams that laugh are less stressed and can face serious issues and seemingly insurmountable obstacles with much more ease. This small proverb, "All work and no play make Jack a dull boy," fits well. If your congregation is in the doldrums, perhaps there is a need to laugh and play. The Mission statement of the congregation I serve has this phrase, "We will rejoice in the Lord." Our humor and joy is rooted in our relationship with Christ.

For instance, Miriam took a tambourine, danced and sang when the Israelites crossed the Red Sea.[163] Miriam's song is a beautiful expression of celebration before God. While faith is a serious matter, there is a time to laugh and celebrate what God has done, is doing, and will do in our lives and congregations. In the opening verse of Psalm 126 God restores the fortunes of Zion. In response to God's work the people respond, "Then our mouth was filled with laughter, and our tongue with shouts of joy." Congregations need to express deep laughter and joy before God. How might your vision or mission express deep joy and celebration before God?

The seventh key of symbolic leadership states that ritual and ceremony renew spirit and reinforce values. People are bombarded daily by events that cause stress. Congregations have the opportunity not only to provide deep joy for parishioners, but also ceremonies and rituals that give meaning to the transitions in life. Religious rituals provide meaning, stability, and security at the deepest level of our existence.

Unfortunately, many people equate rituals with the less intelligent, when in fact all humans engage in some ritual action. Richard Wentz defines ritual in this way, "Ritual is patterned behavior, a set of actions that expresses our thoughts and feelings about existence in a cosmos we are unable to describe or define."[164] Christian worship is a meaningful ritual marked by a set pattern. In it we express our adoration for the eternal God who created a vast and incomprehensible universe. Liturgical worship uses a prescribed pattern similar to Isaiah's vision as recorded in Isaiah chapter 6. For instance, worship is a time of confession, a time to repent, a time to hear the Word of God, and a time to be sent into service. Thus, Isaiah says, "Here am I! Send me."[165]

All of us need meaning, stability, security, and purpose and will seek it even in the most unlikely of places. For instance, one morning while I was leaving the hospital, Bob, an inactive Lutheran (He and his wife had never affiliated with any congregation in our area) greeted me warmly while waiting with his Fox Terrier at the entrance to the hospital. We chatted briefly and he asked if I had seen his wife. Since I did not even know she was hospitalized, I had not. He asked me to wait with him at the entrance of the hospital because his wife was to arrive soon in order to be transported for a test. She exited the hospital by wheelchair and her husband reintroduced me to her. What happened next was nothing less than stunning. I did not receive a hello or any acknowledgement despite her husband's efforts, but rather the lady was enamored by her little dog that begged to jump in her lap. The tiny terrier received all her affections and her attention; I stood there humbled by being less needed than the dog!

Somewhere along the way I cannot help but wonder if her vision of the church was small, not a powerful place of grace and prayer. Apparently the dog provided her more support and love than the congregation to which she once belonged. Why did she reject the church?

Will our congregations be known as disciple - making congregations? Will the vision be so clear that everyone feels welcomed and warmed by God's grace? Or will cats and dogs win the affections of people and preclude their yearning for the community of God's people?

If we are to confront the worldly values espoused by so many and be the church that God calls us to be we need a clear and welcoming vision. St. James Lutheran Church of Sumter adopted the following vision statement, "We are one body, growing in faith, where all are welcome and Jesus is Lord." St. James is one small part of the body of Christ. The church of Jesus Christ extends to every crevice and cranny of the globe. Each congregation needs to see its place in the wider band of all Christian churches and determine its specific vision. Does your congregation offer a strong arm to lift up those trampled under foot by the pressures of life? Does your congregation extend an inviting hand to those reaching for purpose and meaning in life? Can your disciples point out the injustices in our world? Together we are a powerful team with a powerful vision of making disciples.

Numerical measures of success are helpful and fine in their place, but ministry is certainly more than attendance on Sunday morning or the offering totals. Ministry is influencing the world for Jesus Christ and welcoming people into the kingdom of God. Those who aspire to lead in the church are called to build Fifth Frame Christian leadership learning teams. The final chapter is about building a Christian leadership learning team. It will assist your team in utilizing Fifth Frame ideas to broaden your vision for ministry so that all may know Christ's love.

Chapter Six: Questions for Reflection

1. Does your congregation have a statement of vision? Is it displayed prominently, believed passionately, and taught regularly?

2. What identity does your congregation have in your community? What do the people surrounding your church believe and think about your ministry?

3. How might your vision help the congregation see beyond the institutional flaws and conflicts inherent in all churches?

4. Does your congregation have high expectations of its members? If so, is there a document that outlines congregational values and core values?

5. What stories about the birth of your congregation could enable you to tap new energy and create a new or renewed vision?

6. Does your congregation embrace laughter and humor?

7. Discuss your congregation's specific call to ministry. How do you see your congregation in relation to the Christian churches in your area?

Chapter Seven

The Fifth Frame and Christian Leadership Learning Teams

As a young child my Saturday mornings were reserved for the television program "The Lone Ranger." I suppose it had something to do with my father's love for westerns. At any rate, for the longest time I thought of my childhood heroes as stand alone conquerors. Amazingly, I neglected to see that alongside "The Lone Ranger" was his sidekick Tonto. Why is it that we automatically think that heroes operate all by themselves or that leaders stand alone? Sadly, some clergy and lay Christian leaders function as "Lone Ranger" Christians. To whom are they accountable and with whom will they share their burdens and concerns?

Leaders in the Christian church are bombarded with problems and criticisms, most often by the well intentioned. Clearly, Christian leaders need constant support and encouragement. From the very beginning of the biblical narrative God expresses his desire for humans to be in partnership with one another. This begins with the basic unit of the family, "It is not good that the man should be alone."[166] So that they would not be alone, Jesus sent his disciples into mission two by two.[167] God calls leaders so that they might discern and grow their skills within Christian community. A primary task of Fifth Frame Christian leaders is to recognize the need for accountability and support to strengthen our biblical leadership.

This accountability and support can be enhanced by forming Christian leadership learning teams. A learning team is a unique designation first defined by Peter Senge: "Organizations where people continually expand their capacity to create the results they truly desire, where new and expansive patterns of thinking are nurtured, where collective aspiration is set free, and where people are continually learning how to learn together."[168] Christian leadership learning teams are centered in the Fifth Frame; they enhance trust, build community, and strengthen dialogue.

Christian leadership learning teams use the Fifth Frame model as a guide and understand that God is transcendent, having no limits. Some years ago the author J.B. Phillips captivated many with the title of his book; *Your God is too Small.* Like the small crosses that adorn many sanctuaries, are our perceptions and beliefs about God so small that we limit his ability to grow people for service in the kingdom? In contrast, the Fifth Frame congregation continually expands its belief in the miraculous power of God. The transcendent, all-powerful God is the center of our lives as leaders. It is not our leadership desires and wishes that come to fruition, but the will of God. The Christian leader is an instrument of God's grace and power. Through God's power strangers become friends, empty minds are filled with knowledge, seekers grow in faith, members blossom into disciples, and all become one in community.

Christian leadership learning teams work diligently to build a sense of sincere and deep Christian community. For instance, consider what I witnessed at Mepkin Abbey, a Trappist monastery in Moncks Corner, South Carolina. In 1985, I worshiped with the monks six times a day for four days. What happened in one worship service was amazing. As the monks neared the end of the service, they all turned to face the altar (they normally faced one another), bowed their heads, and were completely silent. I imitated their actions and bowed my head wondering just what was happening, until I heard every voice praying in unison, "But deliver us from evil." I realized they were praying the Lord's Prayer during the silence. They demonstrated an amazing unison of prayer.

When a group of people function as a whole, Peter Senge calls this "alignment."[169] Christian leadership learning teams begin by being in alignment in their prayers, their service, their vision and their common commitment to leadership. A Christian leadership learning team is committed to growing all people into Christian leaders who are centered on a transcendent God in relationship with Jesus Christ, equipped through the Holy Spirit, transformed by the Word, called into service, molded into disciples, and humbled by God's power. This is the essence of Fifth Frame leadership teams.

Christian leadership learning teams build trust, one of the foundational elements of Christian community. Trust comes through speaking the truth in love. This means Christian leaders must be open to dialogue and the reality that conflict exists. Though it exists, the church should oppose destructive conflict marked by *ad hominen* attacks and encourage a healthy diversity of ideas and insights about how to do ministry. Senge identifies dialogue as an important element of building a learning team and cites the work of David Bohm who contends it enables participants to access a "larger pool of meaning."[170] While I understand Bohm's concept, Christian leaders' have dialogue within the community of God's people to discern God's will. While disagreements are inevitable, God intends that we discern direction for our congregations in the rough and tumble of community and in our interactions with other Christians. If a person leaves a congregation when disputes arise, will they ever learn deep and forgiving resolution? God speaks through his Word in the context of the community of believers. This means that those who receive a private revelation from God must be willing to submit it to the gathered community for verification.

Clergy and lay leaders know of individuals who contend that God has given them a personal revelation and who work to convince the congregation to endorse the idea. Or as one parishioner put it we do not need any more "committees of one."

A committee of one is one person making an important decision that impacts the entire congregation. Whether it is personal revelation or the committee of one, if the idea or insight is truly of God, dialogue with other Christians can authenticate and discern the decision. This means that a free exchange of ideas must exist without the desire to defend one's position. Christian leadership learning teams help team members be accountable to each other and understand that the Holy Spirit guides all discussions that are informed by scripture. If and when healthy disagreements arise, we know that trust is growing.

Existing structures in congregations such as councils, deacon boards, or vestries may or may not function as learning teams. How might these teams be retooled as leadership learning teams? Patrick Lencioni in his excellent work, *The Five Dysfunctions of a Team,* provides five elements that must be present to build a team. They are; they trust one another, they engage in unfiltered conflict around ideas, they commit to decisions and plans of action, they hold one another accountable for delivering against those plans, and they focus on the achievement of collective results.[171]

Trust is the foundation of team building and exists when the Christian leadership team is willing to be vulnerable and open in sharing conflicting ideas. While this is never easy, the dialogue is about ideas, not personalities. George Manning and Kent Curtis describe four different styles of human relations. They are, "turtle –has little trust and withdraws from others, owl – shows a willingness to listen but is reluctant to share ideas and feelings with others, bull in a china shop – shares ideas and feelings with others but often fails to listen, picture window – is self expressive and receptive to others."[172] Fifth Frame Christian leaders need to be expressive of their ideas and receptive to the ideas of others while recognizing the diversity of the team and believing passionately that the Holy Spirit guides dialogue. If we truly believe God calls people of differing gifts to be the body of Christ, then we need to hear all Christian voices in the community. It is understood that the plumb line of the gospel and the foundation of the Word of God is the standard by which all communications are measured. We need to listen for God's truth in our discussions and dialogues.

Christian leadership learning teams discern God's specific vision for their congregations through dialogue in the Christian community, but dialogue must be saturated with prayer. It is amazing to me that Christian committees and teams would dare to meet or make decisions without first praying. Dr. Haddon Robinson shared a story in a sermon about the Lord's Prayer that he called the pennies game. It is a children's game in which one person places their hand over the hand of another who is holding pennies. The person whose hand is held over the other tries to snatch pennies from the hand below. Dr. Robinson stated that in prayer we go to God to take the pennies (blessings) when we should simply take God's hand. Prayer should never solely be a time to get something from God nor should it feel like a duty, but rather it is an opportunity to hold the hand of our heavenly Father and feel and hear God's truth.

Carol Hymowitz writes about Kent Thiry, chief executive of DaVita Corporation, and his efforts to build a "truth telling culture." He seeks feedback from employees and customers as often as possible and strives to not isolate or distance himself from problems and concerns.[173] Church leaders who choose to close their ears create a secretive and closed culture. The dangers of a non-communicating climate are problems go unmentioned and ultimately unsolved, because it is expected no one will listen.

For instance, a Dilbert cartoon shows Dilbert coming to his boss with a suggestion. In the second frame the boss says, "Give me a minute to install my management listening catheter." In the final frame the boss has a tube stuck to one ear and another tube coming out the opposite ear entering into the trash can.[174] Some congregations may feel as though their leaders do not listen or choose to not hear their concerns. Christian leadership learning teams value genuine and sincere feedback.

A team of leaders is always better than one. I cringe when seminars parade "super" individuals whose congregation grew 35% in the past year across a stage so that others can imitate their success. Congregations can grow numerically by meeting everyone's needs and preaching a gospel of wealth, but we are not called to make people feel good all of the time. While I appreciate the need for us to mentor and identify other leaders, how they lead and by whose power must be equally stressed. It is important to stress the method of leadership and that strong effective leaders are surrounded by support teams. It is counterproductive to turn pastors and other church leaders into celebrities. They are not the source of wise leadership; only God gets the accolades and praise.

One need only read the story of King Uzziah in 2 Chronicles chapter 26. He was blessed with a powerful army and as long as he sought after and feared God, all was well. But then pride became his downfall. He entered the temple and attempted to burn incense, a job reserved for the priests. While in the temple he was stricken with leprosy. Compare this with the call narrative of Isaiah in chapter 6 which begins in this way, "In the year that King Uzziah died..."[175] Perhaps Isaiah communicated by contrast; Uzziah was prideful and it led to his downfall whereas Isaiah was overcome with a deep sense of God's holiness and his unworthiness.

King Uzziah fell out of favor with God when he attempted to do that for which he was not called. Fifth Frame leaders recognize that all people are not gifted in the same way, but that each person is essential in building a leadership team. Learning teams dialogue constantly to build trust, increase accountability, discern leadership gifts and support one another.

Ultimate support comes from Jesus who is the head of the church and from whom all learning teams grow. This means that our image of Jesus as a leader needs to be informed by scripture. All too often our image of Jesus is him caressing and holding a lost lamb. Lesslie Newbigen challenges our stain-glassed image of Jesus to which we have grown accustomed. He suggests that the background for Jesus' parables were probably informed by the texts in Ezekiel. He writes: "The ideal shepherd is the warrior king David, doing justice, punishing the wicked, leading God's people in warfare and in peace."[176] How might this image of Jesus affect our leadership? Shall we dare to see him as the one who does justice, punishes the wicked, and leads people in warfare and peace?

Once in preaching class Dr. Richard Carl Hoefler shared a story about a rural farm family that noticed their youngest child missing after a long day of work in the field. They called her name repeatedly, but she did not respond. Frantically, the family raced into the corn fields to find their child before evening fell. After a long search each family member returned empty handed. Word spread quickly in the small farm community and neighbors came to help. As everyone gathered, the little lost girl's brother suggested that everyone hold hands and walk through the corn field together. Together, while holding hands, they came upon the little girl shriveled up and seriously dehydrated in the middle of a distant corn field.

As we hold hands in faith, Christian teams can reach individuals who are withering and wilting with dehydration. They need the true hydrating water of life, Jesus Christ. Across denominational lines we have a chance to be the body of Christ, to be one church, one voice, one strong force working to impact the world and announce that the Kingdom of God is at hand. Let us build strong leadership teams and send them out searching for the lost and alone and bring them the nourishing love of God. May it be so!

Chapter Seven: Questions for Reflection

1. Reflect on Genesis 2:18. Have you ever felt alone in your congregational leadership? If so, how have you sought the advice and counsel of other Christians?

2. Read Matthew 11:28-30. To whom are you accountable in your congregation? Is there a regular system of reporting and dialogue among leadership? What does Jesus teach us about accountability and sharing our burdens?

3. Discuss among your leadership team the concept of a learning team.

4. Read 1 Corinthians 1:10-13. Does your congregational leadership team function as a community of God's people?

5. How might your leadership team build Christian community?

6. Does a "truth telling culture" exist in your congregation? Is it flavored with God's amazing love?

7. Read Proverbs 11:2. Why is pride so dangerous? Consider this quotation from Reinhold Niebuhr, "But it would be well if the church realized how dangerous power and prestige are, and how easily they corrupt a man's spiritual integrity." [177]

Appendix A

Characteristics, Bible Passages, and Questions

Symbolic – **Persuasion** – A: 2 Corinthians 5:11, B: Deuteronomy 5:1-21, 6:1-9, C: Mark 14:22-25

Political – **Shrewdness** – A: Matthew 10:16, B: Exodus 19: 17-23, C: Mark 6:6b-13

Structural – **Understanding** – A: Proverbs 2:6, B: Numbers 16:1-41, C: Mark 5:1-20

Human Resource – **Compassion** – A: Luke 10:25-37, B: Exodus 32:1-32, C: Mark 5:21-24

1. Read passage "A" assigned for your leadership style. Discuss: What leadership characteristic does this verse/passage describe?
2. Read passage "B" for your style. In this passage, how did Moses demonstrate the bible characteristic applicable to your leadership style?
3. Read passage "C" for your style. In this passage, how did Jesus demonstrate the bible characteristic applicable to your leadership style?

Reconvene, present group results

Appendix B

A Sample Seven Session Christian Leadership Retreat

Goals:
1. To present a model of biblical leadership
2. To strengthen our own concepts of leadership and abilities as leaders using the "Fifth Frame"
3. To consider each gift of leadership and work to build effective leadership teams
4.

Session One
1. Discuss the question, "Who is God?"
2. Read Isaiah 9:6-7. What are other names you use for God?
3. Read Exodus 3:13-15. What does God mean by "I AM?"
4. Read Exodus 33:18-23. Why is Moses forbidden from seeing God's face?
5. Using a dictionary define the word "transcendent."
6. What difference does it make for Christian leadership that God is transcendent?

Session Two
1. Discuss the question, "What is the Word of God?"
2. Is there a distinction between the Word of God and Holy Scripture?
3. What is your congregation's view of Holy Scripture?

4. Does your congregation have a document or doctrinal statement about scripture?

5. Are your leaders familiar with the statement?

6. Read 2 Timothy 3:16-17. What does it mean that scripture is inspired?

7. What does it mean to you that God's Word has power and how is this important to Christian leadership?

Session Three

1. Discuss the question, "What does it mean to be called by God?"

2. Read Exodus 3:1-4:17. What are the objections of Moses? How does God respond?

3. What does it mean to you that God equips those whom he calls?

4. In small groups discuss God's call in your life. How might God use your frailties and faults? What about your congregation?

5. Do you believe God has called you to leadership training? If so, in what way?

Session Four

1. Discuss the question, "What does it mean to be a disciple of Christ?"

2. Read Luke 14:25-33. What possession, habit, or attitude do you need to give to God in order that you might deepen your discipleship? What about your congregation?

3. What spiritual disciplines might you focus on to deepen your relationship with God?

4. Read and meditate on "1 Timothy 6:3-12." Spend time in prayer seeking discernment on "sound teaching."

5. Are you hearing specific discernment about your specific call to leadership in the congregation?

Session Five

1. Discuss the question, "What does it mean to be humble?"

2. Read Romans 12:3. How are we to count others better than ourselves?

3. A seminary president once remarked, "If you think you are humble, they you are not." Do you believe this to be true? Why or why not?

4. In small groups devise a definition of humility. Share with the larger group and discuss.

5. Why should leadership have anything to do with Christian leadership?

Session Six

1. Discuss the question, "What do you believe are the primary characteristics of Christian leadership?

2. Review the leadership characteristics in Chapter three.

3. Read 1 Corinthians 2:1-5. Paul says he came in weakness, fear and trembling. How can leaders persuade when they are weak?

4. What leadership characteristics do you have?

5. What teams might you build so that many characteristics are utilized?

Session Seven

1. Discuss the question, "How can Christian leaders use symbolic, structural, human resource, and political frames or leadership?

2. Using Lee Bolman and Terrence Deal's categories of leadership, what behaviors do you believe best represent you? Your leadership team?

3. How can you build a team with diverse leadership gifts?

Appendix C

Sample Sermons

Sermon One

This sermon seeks to broaden the perspective of our view of Jesus as the Good Shepherd. All too often the view of Jesus as the gentle shepherd caressing the lamb clouds our view of Jesus. He also carries a staff to scare away or fight the wolves. This sermon seeks to redefine our view of Jesus and thus shape concepts of leadership.

Jesus--the Good Shepherd?

What image of God do you hold in your mind's eye? Is it that of a bearded wise old man sitting on a throne? Our images and visualization of God may have a direct impact on our leadership. Consider, for instance your image of Jesus as the Good Shepherd. When you think of Jesus, what image do you see? Naturally, we remember Psalm 23 and we see still water, a true pastoral scene. We might visualize Jesus holding the lamb in his arms. We see him as warm, kind, caring, compassionate, inviting, helpful, and gentle. Gently caressing the lost lamb is what we most often see. What other words might you use?

A church scholar by the name of Lesslie Newbigin wrote these words about Jesus as the Good Shepherd,

> "Let us begin by acknowledging that the figure of the Good Shepherd has been sentimentalized in the course

of church history. One thinks of the stained-glass windows and the pictures in which Jesus is portrayed as a womanish figure apparently caressing a new lamb. We can correct this by reading again the texts in Ezekiel which probably formed the background for Jesus' parable. The figure of the Shepherd there is more like a warrior. The ideal shepherd is the warrior king David, doing justice, punishing the wicked, leading God's people in warfare and in peace."

What are we to make of this image suggested by Newbigin – that of the warrior shepherd? This is challenging to our sensibilities. It is almost as if we were to put an M-16 rifle in our Lord's hands. We would be upset, and so should we. But there is a staff in his hands and it is there for a purpose.

Perhaps we will remember the time when Jesus entered the temple and turned over the tables of the moneychangers. Remember the story in Matthew chapter 21 beginning with verse 12. Jesus enters the temple and drove out the moneychangers. He then speaks to them with these firm words, "My house will be called a house of prayer,' but you are making it a 'den of robbers.'"

Note that Jesus did not have a dialogue or a discussion with the moneychangers. Jesus did not form a committee. Jesus took charge and DROVE THEM OUT. Those who would use the church of Jesus Christ for their own gain will face the strong hand of the Good Shepherd. Jesus drives out the demons of greed and selfish gain.

If that were the only instance in which we see our Lord's firmness we might easily dismiss it, but there is more. Consider the "pleasant" exchange of words with Peter. Remember this conversation?

Matthew 16:21- "From that time on, Jesus began to show his disciples that he must go to Jerusalem and undergo great suffering at the hands of the elders and chief priests and scribes, and be killed, and on the third day be raised. And Peter took him aside and began to rebuke him, saying, "God forbid it, Lord! This must never happen to you." But he turned and said to Peter, "Get behind me, Satan! You are a stumbling block to me; for you are setting your mind not on divine things but on human things." Matthew 16:21-23

Peter has the idea that he knows better than Jesus what Jesus should do. When Jesus shares his mission – suffer, die, be raised; Peter says, God forbid it. How many times do we presume to know better than our Lord what his will should be for OUR LIFE? Do we tell God how to run our lives? Do we tell God how to run his church? Or rather do we completely turn our lives and our congregations over to the direction of Jesus? Do we as Christian leaders really believe in the power of our Messiah?

Jesus turns over tables, calls one of his closest disciples Satan and commands the winds and the waves. Does this Good Shepherd have power? What do you think?

A great windstorm arose, and the waves beat into the boat, so that the boat was already being swamped. But he was in the stern, asleep on the cushion; and they woke him up and said to him, "Teacher, do you not care that we are perishing?" He woke up and rebuked the wind, and said to the sea, "Peace! Be still!" Then the wind ceased, and there was a dead calm. Mark 4:37-39

Jesus has power to command the wind and the waves. When Jesus confronts sin, death and the devil, he is strong. Would we want him to be anything else?

In the 10th chapter of John Jesus says,

"The good shepherd lays down his life for the sheep. He who is a hireling and not a shepherd, whose own the sheep are not, sees the wolf coming and leaves the sheep and flees; and the wolf snatches them and scatters them. I lay down my life for the sheep."

Jesus does not flee when the wolf roams. Jesus does not flee when evil lurks at the door seeking someone to devour. Jesus does not flee when trouble is brewing in our hearts. Jesus is the strong shepherd who willingly stands toe to toe with evil, triumphing time after time.

Where is this evil? Where are the wolves with which we must do battle? Listen to these shocking words from the Apology to the Augsburg Confession: "But why belabor the obvious? If the church, which is truly the kingdom of Christ, is distinguished from the kingdom of the devil, it necessarily follows that since the wicked belong to the kingdom of the devil, they are not the church. In this life, nevertheless, because the kingdom of Christ has not yet been revealed, they are mingled with the church and hold office in the church."

The church is the hot spot where evil and good meet. And so it is our prayer, today and every day that the Good Shepherd, the one who lays down his life for the sheep and the one who confronts the wolves will reside in our lives and stand firmly in our church.

Jesus will come to our churches and lead by picking up his staff. As leaders we should invite the Messiah to cast out the demons of disobedience, cast out the demons of bitterness, cast out the demons of gossip, cast out the demons of division, and cast out the demons that would destroy the mission of our Lord. We need the Good shepherd not only to gently hold us in his arms of mercy but also to drive out that which hinders our relationship with God. Jesus needs to turn over the tables of indifference and apathy and set us on fire.

We pray for the protection of the Good Shepherd knowing that Jesus has all power and can face the power of evil and win. May the Good Shepherd live in us and in this congregation. AMEN

Sermon Two

The following sermon, first preached on Easter morning, stresses the need for individuals to get in the race and hold to the faith. There is responsibility for everyone to lead in the ministry God gave them.

Hold the Baton!

Imagine this morning that you are seated in the stands preparing to watch a relay race. But not just any relay race, but rather the largest and most important relay race in the world. What you see are many runners, a huge track, and batons. The baton, which Webster's dictionary defines as, "a hollow cylinder carried by each member of a relay team and passed to the succeeding runner," is extremely important in the relay race. Each runner must carry the baton and then pass it on to the next runner. The basic instructions to the runner are probably this simple, 1. run the track as quickly as possible, 2. DO NOT DROP THE BATON!, 3. pass on the baton to the next runner. So, here we are you and I watching a relay race.

We have four runners on our team – each representing us. So as in any sporting event we want to cheer our runner on and encourage them. Our four runners, just to make it fun are named, Adam, Brian, Chris, and Doug. A,B,C,D see just so you can remember easily!

The gun fires and all the runners are off. Adam's arms are flailing away, look at him pump those arms. But wait there seems to be a problem, Adam is running in place. He is making a lot of motion, holding pretty firmly to the baton, even breaking a sweat, but he is going NOWHERE and as we like to say, he is going NOWHERE FAST! What in the world will we do? So the coach grabs another runner and takes Adam out of the race.

Finally, our new runner who replaced Adam gets around to Brian. He passes the baton and Brian is off. Great, you see Brian.

Can you see him? He is actually running. Wow, what a relief. He makes the first turn and then the second and he is down the backstretch running hard. And then suddenly, without warning, Brian runs off the track, down the exit, and disappears from the arena. Minutes pass and the coach is hysterical. What will he do? Again, he puts in another runner, who takes the baton dropped by Brian on the way out of the arena. This runner gets all the way around to our original third runner – Chris.

By this time Chris is energized and ready. He takes off with the baton and runs with amazing speed. He makes the first turn but then something happens, he stops walks over to the sidelines where someone offers him a cup of coffee. Chris pauses and drinks the coffee slowly, savoring every drop. The coach yells at the top of his lungs, but it falls on deaf ears. Finally, Chris starts running again and the coach is relieved, but only for a moment. Chris, stops again walks over to another crowd member and drinks a coca cola and begins eating a burger and fries. The coach is hysterical. What is Chris doing? Again, Chris begins his run but again he stops, goes up into the stands and sits to watch a television screen in the press box. What is going on with this guy? Does he not know he is in a race?

Finally, Chris gets around to our fourth runner Doug. Doug takes off and runs his heart out. He makes turn one, then turn two, then the backstretch, then turn three, and finally turn four. Is it possible? Will our fourth runner, our runner, will he make it to the finish line? YES! HE DOES. Doug crosses the finish line and just as quickly is disqualified. WHY? He dropped the baton in turn one and never bothered to pick it back up.

Sadly, you and I return home – we have lost the race. Now wasn't that fun?

Allow me to give some meaning to this race. The baton, if you remember, is extremely important. Listen again to these words from 1 Corinthians 15, "For I handed on to you as of first importance what I in turn received: that Christ died for our sins in accordance with the scriptures, and that he was buried, and that he was raised on the third day in accordance with the scriptures, and that he appeared to Cephas, then to the twelve. Then he appeared to more than five hundred brothers and sisters at one time, most of whom are still alive, though some have died. Then he appeared to James, then to all the apostles."

The baton is the message of salvation, the message of Jesus death, burial, resurrection and appearance. Jesus died. Jesus was buried. Jesus was raised. Jesus appeared to believers.

Adam, our first runner ran in place. He forgot that the baton is not just something we hold in our hands but rather is that which transforms us into people who run a race. There are many who profess faith with their heads but their hearts are far from the work of the kingdom of God. Isaiah 29:13, "The Lord says: "These people come near to me with their mouth and honor me with their lips, but their hearts are far from me." When the baton is passed to you, you have a responsibility to not only carry it but allow it to transform you into a runner, a runner with passion, a runner with courage, a runner with an abiding and deep faith in the power of Jesus Christ.

Our second runner Brian, as you recall, runs out of the arena. He ran off the track. He ignored the basic rules – run the race ON THE TRACK. He decided to believe something else. Who knows just what it was that lured Brian into running out of the arena. Whatever it was Brian chose to ignore the instructions. In the church we call this heresy. Heresy is that which is not in accordance with the scripture. Notice that which the apostle Paul says he "handed on to you." He says it twice, so pay attention, "in accordance with the scriptures..."

Our third runner Chris started strong but then stopped for coffee, then coca-cola burger and fries, then television. Basically, Chris was distracted by that which refreshed. He is akin to those who want something that makes them feel good. It is all about them and what they want – a little refreshment and a little entertainment. Thankfully, Jesus did not choose this path, but rather willingly endured the suffering and humiliation of the cross so that through his death he could accept all the sin of humanity.

Our final runner, Doug, ran well, but did not carry the baton. Perhaps he had heart. Perhaps he had energy. Perhaps he even had dedication, but he forgot that there is a baton to carry. How many of us know our faith well? When was the last time you dusted off the family bible and took it for a spin? When was the last time you read some of those stories you were taught as a child? Do these words really mean something to you? Do you know the story of Jesus salvation for you and all people?

For I would remind you, brothers and sisters, of the good news that I proclaimed to you, which you in turn received, in which also you stand, through which also you are being saved, if you hold firmly to the message that I proclaimed to you – unless you have come to believe in vain. For I handed on to you the baton of salvation!

Jesus died, Jesus was buried, Jesus was raised, Jesus appeared to many! Jesus is ALIVE! Hallelujah!!!

Run the race. Hold the baton. Hold to it firmly. Be transformed. Pass it on! AMEN!!!!

Sermon Three

The following sermon is about casting a vision. God holds the future for believers and congregations. God's vision is for us to plant seeds of love through his son Jesus Christ.

A Vision of Harvest

Did you hear the silly story about the elderly man who lived in the desert? He took a long trip traveling along a mountain road when he came to a tunnel. It was the first time in his life he had seen a tunnel. He stopped his truck, got out, looked for several minutes into the tunnel, and then, got back into his truck. He made a u turn and headed back the way he came. As he headed back he muttered to himself, "I could get in this end of the tunnel O.K. But I could never squeeze this truck through that little opening at the other end."

That is what we call tunnel vision. Tunnel vision is not being able to see beyond a little area. Tunnel vision gives us a narrow perspective. It is the person who sees the trees but cannot take in the forest.

In my July newsletter I wrote about Vision. I shared with you author George Barna's definition of vision. It is, "Vision for ministry is a clear mental image of a preferable future imparted by God to His chosen servants and is based on an accurate understanding of God, self and circumstances." A clear mental image of the future will fuel our growth at St. James. A vision given to us by God will motivate us and give us strengthened purpose. A vision is never narrow; it is always optimistic and hopeful. Vision is that which motivates us as a congregation.

Jesus had a grand vision. He shares it with us today in the parable of the sower. A few seeds fell on good soil. Those seeds brought forth grain, some a hundredfold, some sixty, some thirty. This parable illustrates for us the confidence of God. The seed are sown and even though there are thorns, even though there are rocks, even though there are hard places, some seed will find good soil and it will grow. And not only will this seed grow it will blossom and flourish.

You and I need to see beyond ourselves, beyond our community. We need to see the big picture. The big picture is that God will reap a GREAT HARVEST. Period. The harvest will come and God's harvest will be bountiful. God will succeed in reaching people with the good news of Jesus Christ, his son our LORD. And God will succeed through the seed that you and I sow; so let us sow, let us cast our messages of faith in Christ broad and wide. Let us not worry where it falls. Let us not worry if we are not good at talking to others. Let us not worry that we have limited abilities or limited talents or limited knowledge. THE HARVEST will come and God will bless us.

As a congregation we need to think of ourselves as a newly planted mission; a mission because there are an abundance of people who really do not know Jesus as one who forgives. Let us tell them about Jesus who loves, Jesus who brings healing, Jesus who has compassion for our hurts, Jesus who is our friend, Jesus who is our guide, Jesus who will bring us to eternity.

All of you have a unique story of faith to share. The great challenge before us today is to help new and young Christians see the entire story of God; the Creation, the Fall, the story of the prophets; all that leads us to the wonderful story of Jesus. We will be shallow disciples without it.

Helmut Thielicke, a German theologian, in his comments on young theologians offers this sage advice. "Before the young freshman has really looked at the cornerstone of the biblical story of salvation, for example, the story of creation and the account of the fall, before he has come to know the alpine peaks of the divine thoughts in their majesty, he is made familiar with the mineralogical analyses of that stone. But anybody who studies geological formations on maps and graphs, and learns mineralogical formulae from a set of tables before he ever climbs the Alps, is hardly in a position to comprehend at all what the Alps are." Thielicke is telling us that the young theologian must not succumb to tunnel vision. Worrying over all the little details and not as Thielicke says breathing in the majesty of God on the tops of the ALPS.

Tunnel vision for us would be to fear the future and when we fear what is ahead, we think we can turn back. Ah, but we know that God leads us forward. God has already shown us the future and the future is filled with great possibilities and great potential. The HARVEST will be GREAT.

In a Peanuts comic strip, there was a conversation between Lucy and Charlie Brown. Lucy said that life is like a deck chair. Some place it so they can see where they are going; some place it so they can see where they have been; and some place it so they can see where they are at present. Charlie Brown's reply: "I can't even get mine unfolded."

Shall we unfold the letter of love sent to us in Jesus Christ? And shall we spread the seed? AMEN

Sermon Four
This sermon first preached on Trinity Sunday elaborates on the holiness of God and our unworthiness.

"Four Movements of the Spiritual Life" Isaiah 6:1-8

Ring, Ring, it is your telephone. You answer the phone. It is a voice you do not recognize. But, it is an important call. You are instructed to appear at high noon the next day for a meeting. A meeting you ask. Yes that is correct. Somehow you know that you have to be there. So you ask no more questions. You feel a sense of urgency in being there.

You arrive at the appointed time and the appointed place. There seated around the room you encounter a very strange phenomenon. You see your mother and father, Billy Graham,

Martin Luther, St. Augustine, Mother Theresa, Emperor Constantine, and yes there at the head of the table sits.... Jesus.

What could this be? Imagine for a moment what you must be feeling. Are you overwhelmed, afraid, in awe? What? Is this the judgment day? Could I be asleep?

This little scenario is just a small picture of the emotional surge felt by Isaiah as he experienced the vision of God's holiness. This passage in Isaiah 6:1-8 is often noted as Isaiah's call. This passage conveys four movements that could be characterized as movements of the spiritual life.

If you are looking for a key to spiritual growth then look no further than right here. First, there is the mighty presence of the HOLY God. Second, there is the painful awareness of our UNHOLINESS. Third, there is FORGIVENESS. Fourth, there is the SENDING.

Join me in a quick journey through the spiritual movement of Isaiah; a spiritual growth that also applies to you and me. This visionary ecstatic experience is real. Isaiah enters the temple and there he sees the Seraphim. The Seraphim is a heavenly being, an angel with six wings. This creature is mentioned only HERE in the entire O.T.

This unearthly creature covers its face with two wings and its feet with two wings. God is HOLY! Even the angelic being, the seraphim, mentioned only here in the entire bible, must cover his face and feet (a reference to nakedness and thus a sense of shame.)

We go about our lives day in and day out oblivious, so much of the time, to the presence of the HOLY! The whole earth is full of God's glory. Our awareness of God's HOLINESS directly impinges upon our awareness of our UNHOLINESS. We can never experience any real spiritual growth until we are stricken down, made painfully aware of our shameful and sinful state. We are not the center of the universe. We are not indispensable. We did not create ourselves. We are filthy and unclean. And we will never fully embrace that nor come to the full awareness of our total depravity until we encounter the HOLY! God is HOLY. God created out of nothing. God existed before all matter. God existed before all things. God is all knowing, all present, all-powerful!

Awareness and Experience of the HOLY drives us to the Experience of our UNHOLINESS. I need to be fixed because I am broken. Many people walk our streets thinking – I am doing just fine thank you. I am a GOOD person. Oh how insidious is that lie. If we say we have no sin we deceive ourselves and the truth is NOT in us. But notice, please, that we do not come to the awareness of our brokenness by beating ourselves up or by a self talk of, "You are a filthy worthless human being." NO, we come to the awareness of our total sinfulness when we ENCOUNTER and EXPERIENCE GOD.

A local "celebrity" cried on the front page of the Item ashamed of what he had done in the much - publicized District 17 scandal. Later, this same individual filed a lawsuit. This is not intended as a judgment of anyone's character, but can someone truly sorry for sin turn around and file a lawsuit of the likes of which we have seen in this case? A true encounter with the HOLY means forgiveness. And forgiveness only comes when one is truly aware of one's sinfulness.

Too many times we think justice is a slap on the wrist. Jesus bore the penalty for our filth and it was no slap on the wrist. It was death on the cross. The HOLY God placed on the shoulders of his ONLY SON the entire filth and unholiness of the world. Every time we do wrong, we drive a nail into the body of our Lord Jesus Christ!

Isaiah said, "Woe is me! For I am lost; for I am a man of unclean lips, and I dwell in the midst of a people of unclean lips; for my eyes have seen the KING, the LORD of HOSTS! He is aware of his unholiness because he is experiencing the HOLINESS of GOD!

Finally, the fourth movement of Isaiah's spiritual growth is the SENDING. Here I am Send Me! Would that more people respond in such straightforward ways to the call of God as issued through the body of Christ – which is the CHURCH! But too often our focus is in the wrong place. We focus on prodding people to DO something when we must first talk about the BEING! We are children of God.

We need not talk about our gifts for service; this is merely one small part of our SENDING. God can call whomever God wants; to do whatever GOD wants! PERIOD. If God wants to use someone with a speech impediment to preach then GOD will do it.

Exodus 4:10-14 "But Moses said to the LORD, "O my Lord, I have never been eloquent, neither in the past nor even now that you have spoken to your servant; but I am slow of speech and slow of tongue." Then the LORD said to him, "Who gives speech to mortals? Who makes them mute or deaf, seeing or blind? Is it not I, the LORD? Now go, and I will be with your mouth and teach you what you are to speak." But he said, "O my Lord, please send someone else." Then the anger of the LORD was kindled against Moses and he said, "What of your brother Aaron, the Levite? I know that he can speak fluently; even now he is coming out to meet you, and when he sees you his heart will be glad."

The SENDING comes from God. We are SENT after we experience God. That is to say we cannot offer true service in the CHURCH unless and until we ENCOUNTER and

EXPERIENCE GOD. Worship is one place where we can Experience God in all of HIS power, might, and HOLINESS.

SENDING is response. SENDING is Stewardship. And it all begins with GOD. Look not first to your gifts, talents, and treasures...look first to GOD and GOD'S HOLINESS. You and I are unworthy to stand before God let alone be sent by God, BUT through the sacrifice of Jesus you and I are invited!

You are Called, You are Cleansed and You are Sent by God!

Bibliography

Allit, Patrick. *The Great Courses: American Religious History,* Chantily: The Teaching Company, 2005

Barna, George. *The Church Today: Insightful Statistics and Commentary*. Glendale: Barna Research Group, 1990.

Baron, David. *Moses on Management: 50 Leadership Lessons from the Greatest Manager of All Time.* New York: Pocket Books, 1999.

Becker, Nancy Jane. "Implementing Technology in Higher Education: The Leadership Role and Perspectives of the Chief Information Officer." Diss. Columbia University Teachers College, 2000. DAI 60/07: 2395.

Bennis, Warren. *Why Leaders Can't Lead*. San Francisco: Jossey Bass, 1989.

Bennis, Warren and Burt Nanus. *Leaders: The Strategies for Taking Charge*. New York: Harper and Row, 1985.

Berger, Peter. "Reflections of An Ecclesiastical Expatriate." *Christian Century*, 24 October 1990, Volume 107.

Boese, Neal and Patricia Haller. *Opening Your Spiritual Gifts.* Chicago: ELCA Education and Evangelism Team of the Division for Congregational Ministries, 2001. ELCA Distribution Service.

Bohrod, Aaron. "The Story of Religions in America: The Lutherans." *Look*, 1 April 1958, 76.

Boice, James Montgomery. *Ordinary Men Called by God: A Study of Abraham, Moses and David*. Grand Rapids: Kregel Publications, 1982.

Bolman, Lee G., and Terrence E. Deal. "Leadership and Management Effectiveness : A Multi – Frame, Multi – Sector Analysis." *Human Resource Management*, Winter 1991: 509-534.

_____. *Leading with Soul*. San Francisco: Jossey-Bass, 1995.

_____. "Looking For Leadership: Another Search Party's Report." *Education Administration Quarterly*, February 1994: 77-97.

_____. *Reframing Organizations: Artistry, Choice and Leadership*. San Francisco: Jossey-Bass, 1991.

Bonhoeffer, Dietrich. *The Cost of Discipleship*. Revised. New York: Macmillan, 1949.

Braaten, Carl and Robert Jensen, ed. *Christian Dogmatics*. Vol. 2, Philadelphia: Fortress, 1984.

Brekke, Milo, and Merton P. Strommen, Dorothy Lowe Williams. *Ten Faces of Ministry: Perspectives on Pastoral and Congregational Effectiveness Based on a Survey of 5000 Lutherans*. Minneapolis: Augsburg, 1979.

Bromiley, Geoffrey W. *Theological Dictionary of the New Testament. Abridged in One Volume*, Gerhard Kittel and Gerhard Friedrich ed. Grand Rapids: Eerdmans, 1985.

Burks, Tom Dean. "The Use of Organizational Frames in Leadership Development." Diss. Peabody College for Teachers of Vanderbilt University, 1992. DAI 53-05A: 1413.

Buttrick, George Arthur ed. *The Interpreter's Dictionary of the Bible*, Vol. 2 Nashville: Abingdon Press, 1962.

Carey, George. *Canterbury Letters to the Future*. Harrisburg: Morehouse, 1998.

Carter, Richard Wesley. "Presidential Leadership Teams: Leadership Styles At Public Universities in Illinois." Diss. Purdue University, 1995. DAI 56-09A: 3409.

Childress, Georgia Pearl Esters. "An Exploratory Study of Leadership Orientation Frames of U.S. Based Japanese and American Leaders in the Automotive Manufacturing Industry." Diss. Peabody College of Vanderbilt University, 1994.

Cimino, Richard ed. *Lutherans Today: American Lutheran Identity in the 21ˢ Century*. Grand Rapids: Eerdmans, 2003.

Davis, Thelma Irene. "The Ways Administrators Work: A Study of the Theoretical Frames of Leadership used by Female and Male Secondary School Principals in Pennsylvania." Diss. Temple University, 1996. DAI 57-06A: 2287.

Dilenschneider, Robert L. *Lessons in Leadership: Moses CEO*. Beverly Hills: New Millenium Press, 2000.

Dulles, Avery. *Models of the Church*. Expanded Edition. New York: Image Doubleday, 1987.

Durocher, Elizabeth Antionette. "Leadership Orientations of School Administrators: A Survey of Nationally Recognized School Leaders." Diss. Columbia University Teachers College, 1995. DAI 57-02A: 525.

Ellison, H.L. *The Daily Study Bible Series*, ed. John C.L. Gibson, Exodus Philadelphia: Westminster, 1982.

Ford, Leighton. *Transforming Leadership: Jesus' Way of Creating Vision, Shaping Values and Empowering Change*. Downers Grove: Intervarsity Press, 1991.

Foss, Michael. *Power Surge*. Minneapolis: Fortress Press, 2000.

Foster, Richard J. *Celebration of Discipline*. San Francisco: Harper and Row, 1978.

Frick, Deborah R. "A Causal-Comparative Study of the Leadership Orientation Frames of Superintendents and Their Perceptions About Educational Change." Diss. University of La Verne, 1996 DAI 57-04A: 1412.

Fretheim, Terence E. *Exodus – Interpretation: A Bible Commentary for Teaching and Preaching*. Louisville: John Knox Press, 1991.

Gall, Meredith D., Walter R. Borg and Joyce P. Gall. *Educational Research: An Introduction*, Sixth Edition, New York: Longman, 1996.

Gardner, John W. *On Leadership*. New York: The Free Press, 1990.

Gaustad, Edwin S. and Mark A. Noll, Eds. *A Documentary History of Religion in America to 1877*, 3rd Edition. Grand Rapids: Eerdmans, 2003

Hall, A.J. "Reflections: The Stories and Images of Women Leaders."Diss. Vanderbilt University, 1992.

Harlow, Janice Heim. "Educational Leadership: A Frame Analysis." Diss. Seattle University, 1994. DAI 55-08A: 2227.

Hasenhuttl, Gotthold. Gregory Baum and Andrew Greeley ed. *The Church as Institution*. New York: Herder and Herder, 1974.

Haugk, Kenneth C. *Antagonists in the Church: How to Identify and Deal With Destructive Conflict.* Minneapolis: Augsburg, 1988.

Heimovics, Richard D. and Robert D. Herman, Carole L. Jurkiewicz. "Executive Leadership and Resource Dependence in Nonprofit Organizations: A Frame Analysis." Public Administration Review 53 (1993):419 -427.

Hendrix, Scott. *The Call.* Lutheran Theological Southern Seminary Library, Lutheran Theological Southern Seminary, Columbia, 1976.

Huey, John and Sam Walton. *Sam Walton: Made in America.* New York: Doubleday, 1992.

Innskeep, Kenneth W. The Context for Mission and Ministry in the E.L.C.A., Department for Research and Evaluation. www. Elca.org/planning/contextual research, accessed 29 September, 2003.

Jensen, Rod. "Luther Leadership: A 16th Century Model for 21st Century Organizational Leaders." Ed. D. diss., Pepperdine, 2001.

Johnson, Benton. Dean R. Hoge and Donald A. Luidens. "Mainline Churches: The Real Reason for Decline," *First Things*, March 1993.

Kelley, Dean M. *Why Conservative Churches are Growing: A Study in Sociology of Religion.* New York: Harper and Row, 1972.

Kniewel, Victoria Spirko. "Leadership Orientation of Principals and Teacher Participation in Decision-Making." Diss. Fordham University, 1999. DAI 60-09A: 3219.

Klaas, Alan and Cheryl. *Clergy Shortage Study.* Smithville: Mission Growth Publishing, 1998.

Koch, Richard. *Moses on Leadership or Why Everyone is a Leader*. Oxford: Capstone Publishing Limited, 1999.

Leith, John H. *Crisis in the Church: The Plight of Theological Education*. Louisville: John Knox Press, 1997.

Lencioni, Patrick. *The Five Dysfunctions of a Team*. San Francisco: Jossey-Bass, 2002

Lewis, Phillip V. Transformational Leadership: A New Model for Total Church Involvement. Nashville: Broadman and Holman, 1996.
Luther, M. Vol. 17: *Luther's works, Lectures on Isaiah: Chapters 40-66*. J. J. Pelikan, H. C. Oswald & H. T. Lehmann, Ed. Luther's Works (Is 55:10). Saint Louis: Concordia Publishing House, 1999, c1972.

Martinez, Richard Stephen. "Self and Administrative Designee Perceptions Of Leadership Orientations of Elementary Principals who have and have Not Completed the California School Leadership Academy." Diss. University of La Verne, 1996. DAI 57-08A:3343.

Manning, George and Kent Curtis. *Communication: The Miracle of Dialogue*. Cincinnati: South-Western Publishing Co., 1988

McCartney-Infelise, Roberta Maurene. "A Study of the Leadership Orientations of MAIS School Directors and a Comparison of their Leadership Orientations with those of Small School District Superintendents in California." Diss. University of La Verne, 1999. DAI 60-05A: 1411.

Metze, Tony Allen. "Multi-Frame Leadership with E.L.C.A. South Carolina Clergy." Diss. Gordon-Conwell Theological Seminary, 2005.

Miro, Arlene Mirabelli. "A Comparative Study of Leadership Orientation Frames Between Public High School Principals Serving in Schools that Applied and did not Apply for California Senate Bill 1274 Restructuring Grants." Diss. University of La Verne, 1993. DAI 55-05A: 1158.

Nelson, E. Clifford. *The Lutherans in North America.* Revised Edition. Philadelphia: Fortress Press, 1980.

Newbigin, Lesslie. *The Good Shepherd: Meditations on Christian Ministry In Today's World.* Grand Rapids: Eerdmans, 1977.

Niebuhr, Reinhold. *Leaves from the Notebook of a Tamed Cynic.* Louisville: Westminster/John Knox, 1980.

Niebuhr, Richard H. *The Purpose of The Church and Its Ministry.* New York: Harper and Row, 1956.

Niehaus, Jeffrey J. *God at Sinai Covenant & Theophany in the Bible and Ancient Near East.* Grand Rapids: Zondervan, 1995.

Nineham, D.E. *Pelican Commentary on Saint Mark's Gospel.* Philadelphia: Westminster, 1963.

Onnen, Melanie K. "The Relationship of Clergy Leadership Characteristics To Growing or Declining Churches." Diss. University of Louisville, 1987. DAI 49-05A: 1174.

Peasley, Robert Bruce. "The California School Leadership Academy: Its Effects on the Leadership Orientations of California Secondary Principals." Diss. University of La Verne, 1992. DAI 53-12A: 4158.

Posner, George J. and Alan Rudnitsky. *Course Design: A Guide to Curriculum Development for Teachers.* Fourth Edition. New York: Longman, 1994.

Redman, Margaret Deal. "A Comparative Study of The Leadership Orientation Frames of Administrators in Private Japanese and American Institutions of Higher Education (Private Institutions)." Diss. University of La Verne, 1991. DAI 52-07A: 2431.

Rivers, Peggy G. "A Frame Analysis of Principals' Leadership Orientations." Diss.University of Central Florida, 1996.

Saarinen, Martin F. *The Life Cycle of a Congregation.* Washington: Albin Institute, 1986.

Schweizer, Eduard. *The Good News According to Mark.* Atlanta: John Knox Press, 1970.

Senge, Peter. *The Fifth Discipline: The Art and Practice of the Learning Organization.* New York: Currency Doubleday, 1990.

Sevig, Julie B. "State of Congregations: Committed and Challenged." *The Lutheran,* January 2004, 33.

Shawchuck, Norman, and Gustave Rath. *Benchmarks of Quality in the Church.* Nashville: Abingdon, 1994.

Sittler, Joseph. *The Doctrine of the Word.* Philadelphia: Muhlenberg, 1948.

Somervill, Charles. *Leadership Strategies for Ministers.* ed. H. Wayland Cummings. Philadelphia: Westminster, 1987.

Stott, John. *Basic Christian Leadership: Biblical Models of Church, Gospel and Ministry.* Downers Grove: Intervarsity Press, 2002.

Tanner, Daniel. Laurel Tanner. *Curriculum Development: Theory Into Practice.* New York: Macmillan Publishing, 1975.

Tappert, Theodore G. ed. *Book of Concord.* Philadelphia: Fortress, 1959.

Tobe, Dorothy Echols. "The Development of Cognitive Leadership Frames Among African American Female College Presidents." Diss. Columbia University Teachers College, 1999. DAI 60-07A: 2300.

Walker, Decker F. Jonas F. Soltis. *Curriculum and Aims*, ed. Jonas F. Soltis, Second Edition - Thinking About Education Series, New York: Teachers College Press, 1992.

Wilkes, C. Gene. *Jesus on Leadership.* Wheaton: Tyndale, 1998.

Wentz, Richard. *American Religious Traditions: The Shaping of Religion in the United States,* Minneapolis: Fortress, 2003.

Woolfe, Lorin. *Leadership Secrets From The Bible: From Moses to Matthew Management Lessons For Contemporary Leaders.* New York: MJF Books, 2002.

Zikmund, Barbara Brown, and Adair T. Lummis, Patricia M.Y. Chang. "Women, Men and and Styles of Clergy Leadership." *Christian Century* 115 (1998): 478 -486.

Endnotes

1. Herb Miller, *The Parish Paper: Ideas and Insights For Active Congregations,* October , 2005

2. This number represents the total of all major Lutheran bodies in the United States in 1958

3. Aaron Bohrod, "The Story of Religions in America -The Lutherans," *Look*, 1 April 1958, 76

4. Dean M. Kelley, *Why Conservative Churches are Growing: A Study in Sociology of Religion*, (New York: Harper and Row, 1972)

5. Benton Johnson, Dean R. Hoge, and Donald A. Luidens, "Mainline Churches: The Real Reason for Decline," *First Things*, March 1993, 15

6. Ibid.

7. Herb Miller, The Parish Paper, August 2005

8. Ibid.

9. Michael Foss, *Power Surge,* (Minneapolis: Fortress Press, 2000), 15

10. H. Richard Niebuhr, *The Purpose of The Church and Its Ministry*, (New York: Harper and Row, 1956), 55

11. Edwin S. Gaustad and Mark A. Noll, Eds. *A Documentary History of Religion in America to 1877, 3rd Edition.* (Grand Rapids: Eerdmans, 2003), 118-119

12. Ibid.

13. Richard E. Wentz, *American Religious Traditions- The Shaping of Religion in the United States,* (Minneapolis:Fortress Press, 2003), 194

14. Robert Bacher and Kenneth Inskeep, *Chasing Down A Rumor-The Death of Mainline Denominations,* (Minneapolis: Augsburg –Fortress, 2005), 176

15. Warren Bennis, *Why Leaders Can't Lead,* (San Francisco: Jossey-Bass, 1989), 65

16. Kenneth W. Innskeep, The Context for Mission and Ministry in the Evangelical Lutheran Church in America, www.elca.org/planning/contextualresearch , accessed 29 September, 2003, 25

17. Robert Bacher and Kenneth Innskeep, *Chasing Down A Rumor – The Death of Mainline Denominations,* (Minneapolis: Augsburg, 2005), 86

18. Inskeep, The Context for Mission and Ministry in the E.L.C.A., 25

19. The E.L.C.A. Department of Research and Evaluation, Chicago Illinois, 2003

20. Julie B. Sevig, "State of Congregations: Committed and Challenged," *The Lutheran,* January 2004, 33

21. Michael Foss, *Power Surge,* (Minneapolis: Fortress Press, 2000)

22. Ephesians 4:12 (R.S.V.)

23. John W. Gardner, *On Leadership,* (New York: The Free Press, 1993), 1

24. Warren Bennis and Burt Nanus, *Leaders: The Strategies for Taking Charge,* (New York: Harper and Row, 1985), 2

25. It should be noted that Wal-Mart has encountered a host of publicity problems in the last few years many of which occurred after the death of Sam Walton in 1992

26. John Huey and Sam Walton, *Sam Walton: Made in America,* (New York: Doubleday, 1992), 246

27. Jack Welch, *Wall Street Journal,* 23 January 2004, A14

28. Warren Bennis, *Why Leaders Can't Lead,* (San Francisco: Jossey Bass, 1989), 18

29. Kenneth W. Innskeep, The Context for Mission and Ministry in the Evangelical Lutheran Church in America, www.elca.org/planning/contextualresearch , accessed 29 September, 2003, 25

30. Ibid., 24

31. Ibid., 26

32. Avery Dulles, *Models of The Church,* (Garden City : Image Books, 1987)

33. Lee Bolman and Terrence Deal, *Reframing Organizations,* (San Francisco: Jossey-Bass, 1991), 5

34. Ibid., 27

35. Peter Senge, *The Fifth Discipline: The Art and Practice of the Learning Organization,* (New York: Doubleday, 1990), 8

36. Douglas John Hall, *Why Christian? For Those on The Edge of Faith,* (Minneapolis: Augsburg Fortress, 1998), p. 123

37. Theodore G. Tappert, Trans. and Ed. *The Book of Concord,* (Philadelphia: Fortress Press, 1959), p. 171

38. Mark Chavez, Network News, Volume 7, Issue 2, March-April 2006, p. 7

39. Peter Senge, The Fifth Discipline, page 193

40. For help in clarifying decisions regarding worship changes leaders would do well to read the work of Marva Dawn, A Royal Waste of Time.

41. Ibid., 445

42. Ibid., 12

43. George Barna Research Group, *The Church Today: Insightful Statistics and Commentary,* (Glendale, CA: 1990), 42

44. Peter Cartwright, *Autobiography of Peter Cartwright* (New York: Nelson and Phillips) Permission: Northern Illinois University, 80

45. 2 Peter 1:5-8 (N.R.S.V.)

46. Ephesians 4:11-13

47. I know this sounds impossible to believe but it really happened!

48. Tony A. Metze, *Multi-Frame Leadership with South Carolina E.L.C.A. Clergy,* (Charlotte: Gordon-Conwell Theological Seminary, Diss., 2005)

49. Lee Bolman and Terrence Deal, *Reframing Organizations,* (San Francisco: Jossey Bass, 1991), 15

50. Charles Somervill, *Leadership Strategies for Ministers,* (Philadelphia: Westminster, 1987)

51. Decker F. Walker, Jonas F. Soltis, *Curriculum and Aims,* ed. Jonas F. Soltis, Second Edition - Thinking About Education Series, (New York: Teachers College Press, 1992), 55

52. Ibid., 56

53. Daniel Tanner, Laurel Tanner, *Curriculum Development: Theory Into Practice ,* (New York: Macmillan Publishing, 1975), 56

54. George J. Posner and Alan Rudnitsky, *Course Design: A Guide*

to Curriculum Development for Teachers, Fourth Edition (New York: Longman, 1994), 8

55. Lee Bolman and Terrence Deal, *Reframing Organizations,* (San Francisco: Jossey Bass, 1991), 324

56. Ibid., 323

57. George Carey, *Canterbury Letters to the Future*, (Harrisburg: Morehouse, 1998), 121

58. Scott Hendrix, *The Call*, (LTSS: unpublished paper, 1976), 12

59. Acts 2:36 (R.S.V.)

60. John H. Leith, *Crisis in the Church :The Plight of Theological Education,* (Louisville: Westminster John Knox Press, 1997), 41

61 Ibid., 42

62 Ibid., 43

63. George Arthur Buttrick, ed., *The Interpreter's Dictionary of the Bible,* vol. 2 (Nashville: Abingdon Press, 1962), 419

64. Hymn # 526, Lutheran Book of Worship

65. Ibid., 424

66. Exodus 3:5 (N.A.S.)

67. Jeffrey J. Niehaus, *God at Sinai Covenant and Theophany in the Bible and Ancient Near East,* (Grand Rapids: Zondervan, 1995), 186

68. Ibid., 188

69. Terence E. Fretheim, *Exodus– Interpretation A Bible Commentary for Teaching and Preaching,* (Louisville: John Knox Press, 1991), 52

70. Peter J. Gomes, *The Good Book- Reading The Bible With Mind And Heart,* (New York: William Morrow, 1996), 3

71. Robert G. Torbet, *A History of the Baptists,* (Valley Forge: Judson Press, 1973), 513

72. Presbyterian Church USA, *The Confession of Faith of the Presbyterian Church in the United States,* (Atlanta: John Knox Press, 1976), 27

73. Book of Discipline - United Methodist Church, (Nashville: United Methodist Publishing House, 2004), 78

74. E.L.C.A. Model Constitution for Congregations, Chapter 2, 2.02C

[75]. Book of Concord-Formula of Concord, Epitome Part 1, (Minneapolis:Augsburg Fortress, 1995)

[76]. Mike Kimble, Conversation at Mike's Light and Magic Shop, Barnyard Flea Market- Lexington, S.C. 31 July 2004

[77]. Joseph Sittler Jr., *The Doctrine of The Word*, (Philadelphia: Muhlenberg Press, 1948), 16

[78]. 2 Timothy 3:16 (C.E.V.)

[79]. Isaiah 55:11 (R.S.V.)

80. Luther, M. (1999, c1972). Vol. 17: *Luther's works, vol. 17: Lectures on Isaiah: Chapters 40-66*, (J. J. Pelikan, H. C. Oswald & H. T. Lehmann, Ed.). Luther's Works (Is 55:10). Saint Louis: Concordia Publishing House.

[81]. Frank Honeycutt, *Preaching to Skeptics and Seekers*, (Nashville: Abingdon Press, 2001), 23

[82]. Carl Braaten and Robert Jensen, *Christian Dogmatics*, Vol. 2, *"The Biblical Understanding of the Word of God"*, Hans Schwarz, (Philadelphia: Fortress Press, 1984), 262

[83.] Luther, M. (1999, c1958). Vol. 40: Luther's works, vol. 40: Church and Ministry II (J. J. Pelikan, H. C. Oswald & H. T. Lehmann, Ed.). Luther's Works (Vol. 40, Page 21). Philadelphia: Fortress Press.

[84]. Terence E. Fretheim, *Exodus – Interpretation A Bible Commentary for Teaching and Preaching*, (Louisville: John Knox Press, 1991), 56

[85]. H.L. Ellison, *The Daily Study Bible Series*, ed. John C.L. Gibson, Exodus (Philadelphia: Westminster, 1982), 16

[86]. Exodus 4:13 (R.S.V.)

[87]. Judges 6:12 (R.S.V.)

[88]. Isaiah 6:5 (R.S.V.)

[89]. Jeremiah 1:5 (R.S.V.)

[90]. Acts 9:1 (R.S.V.)

[91]. Via De Cristo is a spiritual empowerment and renewal weekend.

[92]. Exodus 4:1 (R.S.V.)

[93]. Exodus 17:11 (R.S.V.)

[94]. 1 Samuel 13:13 (R.S.V.)

95. 1 Kings 12 (R.S.V.)

96. Tappert, T. G. (2000, c1959). The book of concord: The confessions of the evangelical Lutheran church (The Confession of Faith: 2, XIV). Philadelphia: Fortress Press.

97. Dietrich Bonhoeffer, *The Cost of Discipleship,* revised ed. (New York: Macmillan, 1949), 64

98. Ibid., 47

99. Richard Foster, *Celebration of Discipline,* (San Francisco: Harper and Row, 1978), 6

100. Michael Foss, *Power Surge,* (Minneapolis: Fortress Press, 2000)

101. John 15:5 (R.S.V.)

102. Acts 21:4 (R.S.V.)

103. Acts 22:18 (R.S.V.)

104. James Montgomery Boice, *Ordinary Men Called by God: A Study of Abraham, Moses and David,* (Grand Rapids:Kregel Publications, 1998), 57

105. Phillip Lewis, *Transformational Leadership,* (Nashville: Broadman and Holman, 1996), 13

106. C. Gene Wilkes, *Jesus on Leadership,* (Wheaton: Tyndale, 1998) , 13

107. Ibid., 11

108. Mark 10:35-37 (C.E.V.)

109. Reinhold Niebuhr, *Leaves from the Notebook of a Tamed Cynic,* (Louisville: John Knox, 1929), 97

110. Rod Jensen, "Luther Leadership: A 16th Century Model for 21st Century Organizational Leaders," (Ed. D Diss. Pepperdine, 2001), 109

111. Ibid., 111

112. Lorin Woolfe, *Leadership Secrets From The Bible From Moses to Matthew – Management Lessons for Contemporary Leaders,* (New York: MJF Books, 2002), xi

113. John Stott, *Basic Christian Leadership: Biblical Models of Gospel and Ministry,* (Downers Grove: Intervarsity, 2002), 114

114. Warren Bennis, *Why Leaders Can't Lead,* (San Francisco: Jossey-Bass, 1989), 118

115. Numbers 12:3 (N.A.S.)

116. Philippians 2:8-9 (C.E.V.)

117. Romans 12:3 (R.S.V.)

118. 2 Corinthians 5:11 (R.S.V.)

119. Acts 18:4 (R.S.V.)

120. 1 Corinthians 2:1-5 (R.S.V.)

121. Patrick Allit, *The Great Courses: American Religious History,* (Chantily Va.: The Teaching Company), Lecture 16

122. Random House, Webster's College Dictionary (1997), s.v. "Shrewd."

123. Geoffrey W. Bromiley, *Theological Dictionary of the New Testament,* Abridged in One Volume, Gerhard Kittel and Gerhard Friedrich eds. (Grand Rapids: Eerdmans, 1985), 1279

124. Luke 16:8 (R.S.V.)

125. Matthew 10:16 (N.A.S.)

126. John Killinger, *Leadership*, "Pastoring is Political- Deal with it." Spring 2006, p. 38

127. 1 Kings 3:9 (R.S.V.)

128. Proverbs 2: 6 (R.S.V.)

129. I secured this quotation from a sermon by Dr. Richard Carl Hoefler

130. Luke 10:25 (R.S.V.)

131. Tappert, T. G. (2000, c1959). *The book of concord: The confessions of the evangelical Lutheran church,* (The Small Catechism: II, 6). Philadelphia: Fortress Press.

132. Adapted from the U.S. Department of Labor Secretary's Commission on Achieving Necessary Skills, What Work Requires of Schools: A SCANS Report for America 2000 (Washington, D.C.: U.S. Government Printing Office, 1992) quoted in Phillip Lewis, *Transformational Leadership,* (Nashville: Broadman and Holman, 1996), 14

133. Warren Bennis and Burt Nanus, *Leaders: The Strategies for Taking Charge,* (New York: Harper and Row, 1985), 2

134. David Baron, *Moses on Management: 50 Leadership Lesons from the Greatest Manager of All Time,* (New York: Pocket Books, 1999), xv

135. Ibid., 33

136. Numbers 10 (R.S.V.)

137. Exodus 30:17 (R.S.V.)

138. Numbers 10:35-36 (R.S.V.)

139. Exodus 18:17-23 (C.E.V.)

140. Numbers 16: 2 (R.S.V.)

141. Baron., *Moses on Management,* 162

142. Exodus 32:30-32 (C.E.V.)

143. Baron, *Moses on Management*, 208

144. D.E. Nineham, *Pelican Commentary on Saint Mark's Gospel,* (Philadelphia: Westminster, 1963), 88

145. Mark 3:4 (C.E.V.)

146. Mark 5:1-20

147. D.E. Nineham, *Pelican Commentary on Mark's Gospel*, 150

148. Mark 5:4 (R.S.V.)

149. Mark 5:19 (R.S.V.)

150. Lee Bolman and Terrence Deal, *Reframing Organizations*, (San Francisco: Jossey Bass, 1991), 262

151. Mark 5:21- 43 (R.S.V.)

152. Eduard Schweizer, *The Good News According to Mark*, (Atlanta: John Knox, 1970), 129

153. 1 Corinthians 1:23 (R.S.V.)

154. Richard Cimino, ed., *Lutherans Today: American Lutheran Identity in the 21st Century*, (Grand Rapids: Eerdmans, 2003), ix

155. Rick Warren, *The Purpose Driven Church,* (Grand Rapids: Zondervan, 1995), 48

156. www.newberry.edu, Student Handbook, accessed 18 May 2006.

157. Peter Berger, "Reflections of An Ecclesiastical Expatriate," *Christian Century*, 24 October 1990, Volume 107, 968

158. Lee Bolman and Terrence Deal, "Looking for Leadership: Another Search Party's Report," *Education Administration Quarterly*, February 1994, Volume 30, 77-97

159. 1 Corinthians 12:14 (R.S.V.)

160. Martin F. Saarinen, *The Life Cycle of A Congregation,* (Washington: Albin Institute, 1986), p.6

161. Robert Hawkins, *Rite of Preparation of a Time Capsule,*

Columbia, South Carolina, Lutheran Theological Southern Seminary, May 13, 2006

162. Susan DeLay, Willow, Volume 13, Issue 1, Page 32

163. Exodus 15:21

164. Richard Wentz, *American Religious Traditions,* (Minneapolis: Fortress Press, 2003), 60

165. Isaiah 6:8 (R.S.V.)

166. Genesis 2:18 (C.E.V.)

167. Mark 6:7

168. Peter Senge, *The Fifth Discipline,* p. 3

169. Ibid. 234

170. Ibid., p. 237, 248

171. Patrick Lencioni, *The Five Dysfunctions of a Team,* (San Francisco: Jossey-Bass, 2002), 189

172. George Manning and Kent Curtis, *Communication: The Miracle of Dialogue,* (Cincinnati: South-Western Publishing, 1988), 91

173. Carol Hymowitz, *In The Lead,* Wall Street Journal – Marketplace, B1, 12 June 2006

174. Dilbert Comic Strip, *The Sumter Item,* 17 June 2006

175. Isaiah 6:1

176. Lesslie Newbigin, *The Good Shepherd: Meditations on Christian Ministry in Today's World,* (Grand Rapids: Eerdmans, 1977), 14

177. Reinhold Niebuhr, *Leaves from the Notebook of a Tamed Cynic,* (Louisville: John Knox, 1929), 97

Made in the USA
Lexington, KY
15 January 2010